# Teknon
## and the
## Champion Warriors

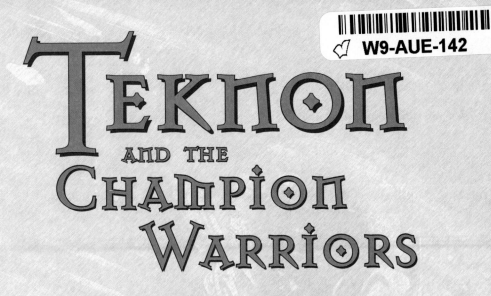

## Mission Guide

### An Interactive Adventure to Explore Courageous Manhood

A companion study guide for
*Teknon and the Champion Warriors*

A *Mentor Guide* for dads and
leaders is also available

*Teknon and the CHAMPION Warriors Mission Guide—Son*

Published by FamilyLife, a division of Campus Crusade for Christ.

Author: Brent Sapp
Senior Editor: Ben Colter
Editorial Team: Stephen W. Sorenson, Anne Wooten, Fran Taylor, David Sims, and Bob Anderson
Illustrator: Sergio Cariello
Designer: Jerry McCall

ISBN 1-57229-246-6
Printed in the United States of America.

NOTE: This book is intended for boys ages 11 to 16. However, it contains some mature subject matter addressing dating, sexual temptation, and pornography.

Dennis Rainey, Executive Director
3900 N. Rodney Parham Road
Little Rock, AR 72212-2441
(501) 223-8663
1-800-FL-TODAY
www.familylife.com

*A division of Campus Crusade for Christ*

*The CHAMPION Training*
*adventure program*
*is dedicated to a pair of champions—*
*my mom and dad*

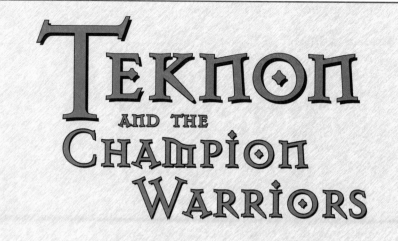

# Teknon AND THE Champion Warriors

## Mission Guide

*An Interactive Adventure to Explore Courageous Manhood*

## Table of Contents

# What is a Champion Warrior?

What comes to mind when you hear the word *warrior*? Today, that word refers to many things, like the road warrior who just invested his entire savings into an overpriced motorcycle and dominates the road. Or the weekend warrior, an overstuffed couch potato who sits in an overstuffed chair, watching whatever stuff ESPN is showing all weekend long. And what comes to mind when you hear the word *champion*? Do you think of the guy who won several gold medals in the Olympics? Or the winner of the Indy 500? Those definitions may be true, but they bear little resemblance to the real warriors and champions of years past.

Many years ago, Native Americans living on the Western plains rode on horseback into battle when they reached their 14th birthday. A boy trained with his father early in life so that he could assume responsibility, take care of others, and, if necessary, fight to protect the safety of the tribe. These sons were more than teenagers; they were young men, each with the *soul of a warrior.*

In July 1776, General George Washington led his 5,000 troops, many under the age of 15, into battle against 25,000 of the finest soldiers Great Britain had to offer. Washington's outnumbered armed forces courageously held their position and played a vital role in gaining the freedom Americans enjoy today. These brave soldiers were more than teenagers; they were young men, each with the *heart of a champion.*

Since those days, many in our society have lost the vision for developing courageous young men. As a result, young men have not been given the responsibility they are capable of taking on. Many have not been challenged to think big thoughts and dream big dreams. How about you? Are you infected with the venom of low expectations or are you setting high standards for yourself? What are your values? What are your goals? Are you living a life full of challenge, adventure, and fulfillment?

How would you like to become a young man with the soul of a warrior and the heart of a champion? You can! Are you ready to begin the quest toward courageous manhood? Are you willing to invest the time and energy? If so, the CHAMPION Training adventure is for you!

Your *Mission Guide* includes 16 CHAMPION Sessions that you will complete and then discuss with your dad or leader over the course of several months. You will probably meet together every other week.

# Elements of a CHAMPION Session

▲ **CHAMPION Characteristics**—One or two key character traits are highlighted for each session.

▲ **Discussion Topics**—Key subjects you will address in the session are summarized.

▲ **Mission Debrief**—Debriefing is a military practice where a soldier recaps his previous mission activities. This section provides you an opportunity to review with your dad the mission that was assigned at your previous session. You will debrief on your critical maneuver, your action point from the Sheet of Deeds, and the new power verse you memorized.

▲ **Reconnaissance**—Reconnaissance (or "recon") is also a military activity in which a soldier explores an area to gather important information for the mission ahead. In this section you and your dad will discuss an episode from *Teknon and the CHAMPION Warriors*.

▲ **Strategy and Tactics**—Strategy refers to the overall planning of a mission. Tactics refers to the methods used to secure the objectives planned out in the strategy. In this section you and your dad will discuss specific CHAMPION characteristics, investigate strategies and tactics from the Bible, and discover how to apply them in your life.

▲ **Your Mission**—At the end of each CHAMPION Session, your dad will assign a mission to you to be completed before the next session. Each mission includes:

■ **Power Verse:** A new Bible verse related to the session for you to memorize.

■ **Critical Maneuver:** A fun, hands-on project or activity for you and your dad to do together to reinforce what you discussed during your session (movies, interviews, tally surveys, Bible discovery, books, and more movies!).

■ **CHAMPION Sheet of Deeds:** You and your dad will agree on an action point that you will begin to apply before the next session and that you will carry on as you develop these deeds for a lifetime as a CHAMPION.

## Get ready for a challenging experience that will change your life!

Courage • Honor • Attitude • Mental Toughness • Purity • Integrity • Ownership • Navigation

# The CHAMPION
## WARRIOR CREED

"If I have the COURAGE to face my fears; HONOR, which I show to GOD[+] and my fellow man; the proper ATTITUDE concerning myself and my circumstances; the MENTAL TOUGHNESS required to make hard decisions; PURITY of heart, mind, and body; the INTEGRITY to stand for what I believe, even in the most difficult situations; effective OWNERSHIP of all that is entrusted to me; and focused NAVIGATION in order to successfully chart my course in life; I will live as a true CHAMPION Warrior, committed to battling evil, and changing my world for GOD's glory."

* Note: In the fiction book, *Teknon and the CHAMPION Warriors*, the Warrior King called Pneuma is a fictional character intended to represent God (Father, Son, and Holy Spirit). For this study, the name Pneuma is only used when referring to the fictional story character.

C OURAGE

H ONOR

A TTITUDE

M ENTAL TOUGHNESS

P URITY

I NTEGRITY

O WNERSHIP

N AVIGATION

# THE CHAMPION CODE

*Character is the moral strength that grows out of our relationship with God.* Personal growth is expressed through the physical, emotional, social, mental, and especially spiritual areas of our lives.*

## Characteristics of a CHAMPION Warrior

### COURAGE

I will cultivate bravery and trust in God. I will break out of my comfort zone by seeking to conquer my fears. I will learn to recover, recover, and recover again.

### HONOR

I will honor God by obeying Him and acknowledging Him as the complete source of my life, both now and through eternity. I will treat my parents, siblings, friends, and acquaintances with respect. I will appreciate the strengths and accept the weaknesses of all my "team members."

### ATTITUDE

I will cultivate a disposition of humility. I will assume a correct and hopeful view of myself as a member of God's family. I will improve my ability to manage anger and discouragement. I will develop and enjoy an appropriate sense of humor.

## Mental Toughness

I will allow God to direct my thinking toward gaining common sense and wisdom. I will use discernment when making hard decisions. I will desire respect from others rather than compromise my convictions for acceptance or approval.

## Purity

I will train myself to keep the temple of my body and mind uncorrupted mentally, emotionally, and physically. I commit to avoid and flee sexual temptation.

## Integrity

I will seek to acquire a clear understanding of who I am in Christ so that I may have a deeper comprehension of what I believe, what I stand for, and how I can live out those convictions in the most difficult circumstances, whether I am alone or with others. I will allow other people to hold me accountable to standards of excellence.

## Ownership

I will apply effective stewardship by using my life and the resources God entrusts to me—including my possessions, time, and talents—for His glory. I will seek contentment in God's provision for my needs. I will learn to practice delayed gratification.

## Navigation

I will allow God to chart my course by accepting my mission from Him, and I will complete that mission by trusting in Him. I will study the Bible, God's Word, so I can know Him better and gain His strength and direction for my life. I will become goal-oriented by learning to focus my attention on completing worthwhile short-term and long-term objectives.

*Note: In the fiction book, *Teknon and the CHAMPION Warriors*, the Warrior King called Pneuma is a fictional character intended to represent God (Father, Son, and Holy Spirit). For this study, the name Pneuma is only used when referring to the fictional story character.

# The Map of the Mission

1
15
2 Kopta
12 13
Northiros
10 11
Hedon Bay
3 Forest of Perasmos
9
14
4
8
Bia
6
7
5 Ergo
Hudor Sea
Sarkinos underground

TEKNON AND THE CHAMPION WARRIORS

# The CHAMPION Sheet of Deeds

Following are my personal action points for each session of my CHAMPION Training.  I will strive to apply these action points during my training adventure and also will make an effort to continue applying them as I seek to grow in godly character for a lifetime of living as a CHAMPION.

Session 1: _____

Session 2a: _____

Session 2b: _____

Session 3: _____

Session 4: _____

Session 5: _____

Session 6: _____

Session 7: _____

Session 8: _____

Session 9: _____

Session 10: _____

Session 11: _____

Session 12: _____

Session 13: _____

Session 14: _____

Session 15: _____

Teknon and the CHAMPION Warriors

# Session 1:
# Destination: Kairos

## CHAMPION Characteristics
**Courage and Navigation**

POWER VERSE: PHILIPPIANS 4:6-7

*Be anxious for nothing, but in everything by prayer and supplication with thanksgiving let your requests be made known to God. And the peace of God, which surpasses all comprehension, will guard your hearts and your minds in Christ Jesus.*

# Discussion Topics

**Preparing for a challenging task**
**Overcoming fear of the unknown**
**Accepting my responsibility and trusting God with the rest**

# Mission Debrief

1. Normally, this section will be used to debrief together about how your mission assignment from the previous session went.

2. Read the CHAMPION Warrior Creed out loud together (see page 5).

# Reconnaissance

1. Carefully review the Map of the Mission on page 8 before beginning this section. Identify where the team is located in episode 1.

2a. What is the CHAMPION definition of **Courage**? Of **Navigation**? (Refer to the CHAMPION Code on page 6.)

_____

_____

_____

_____

_____

*Do the thing you fear, and fear will die.*

Anonymous

3. What opportunity do you think the team has before them on the planet Kairos?

_____

_____

4. Why do you think Teknon was nervous about this mission?

_____

_____

---

## ⊙ptional Questions

5. What kind of training do you think Teknon undertook to prepare for this journey?

_____

_____

6. What do you think Teknon's responsibilities were as he prepared physically, mentally, and spiritually for this mission?

_____

_____

---

7. As the team members stood on the assimilator platform, Kratos said, "... no man is worthy who is not ready at all times to risk body, status, and life itself for a great cause." What do you think Kratos meant? What kind of cause do you think he was talking about?

_____

_____

*There lives in each of us a hero, awaiting a call to action.*

H. Jackson Brown, Jr.

8. How would you apply Kratos' advice to Teknon: "It's all right to be nervous. The trick is learning to channel that nervous energy into something productive"?

_____

_____

_____

# STRATEGY AND TACTICS

1. Review Philippians 4:6-7. What do these verses say about fear or anxiety? How can we face our fears and be at peace?

_____

_____

_____

## TAKING RESPONSIBILITY

In 1917, Will Stoneman gathered all of his courage as he stepped out of the train and into the frigid Canadian air of Winnipeg, Manitoba. He gazed for a moment at the bright lights and endless activity. At age 17, this rugged farm boy from the hills of South Dakota was about to undertake the greatest challenge of his life. In a few short hours, he would begin a 500-mile dog sled race in hopes of winning the $10,000 first prize.

Will needed the money to save his family's farm and pay for his college education. His father had died in a sledding accident only a few weeks earlier, leaving the family without the income from their cabinet-making trade. Now Will was alone in a big city, about to race against the finest sled teams in the world over some of the roughest territory in North America.

What would most teenagers have said if they were faced with Will's challenge?

*What can I do?  I'm just a teenager.*

*It's too late for me to make a difference now.*

*Even if I tried, I'd probably drop out the first day, so I won't bother.*

*I don't have the experience.  Why can't somebody else race for our family?*

Will Stoneman didn't choose to make excuses.  He saw an opportunity to help his family, and he jumped at it.  He courageously took responsibility to compete in a difficult race, even though he had only a month to prepare for it.  During that month, he worked as hard as he could, training himself to race on little food and even less sleep than any of his competitors.  He did everything within his ability to contribute to his family's success.

His determination shocked the entire country when, against incredible odds, he won the race!  His unwillingness to give up, regardless of the circumstances, earned him the nickname "Iron Will."

2.  Read James 1:22-26.  What happens if we only listen to the Word and do nothing?  (See verse 22.)

_____

_____

3.  What will happen to the person who takes responsibility to do what the Word says?  (See verse 25.)

_____

_____

_____

_____

# The Rings of Responsibility

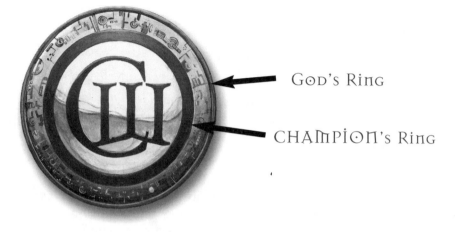

God's Ring

CHAMPION's Ring

## The CHAMPION's Ring

Notice that the Hoplon shield has two rings on it. These circles represent the CHAMPION Warrior's Rings of Responsibility in life. The inner ring is the CHAMPION's Ring, which symbolizes the behaviors and activities in which the CHAMPION can make a difference by obeying God. Inside this ring, a CHAMPION completes his responsibilities without grumbling and without blaming other people for the choices he makes.

A CHAMPION regularly reads the Bible and prays for direction so that he can know how God wants him to think and act. He trusts God to give him the power to make the best choices, while at the same time taking responsibility to do everything he can to live like a CHAMPION.

When we obey God and courageously take responsibility for our choices and actions, we move a step closer toward becoming CHAMPIONs.

4. What are some behaviors and activities that should go into the CHAMPION's Ring?

_____

_____

_____

5. In what areas do you need to assume more responsibility in your life? Be specific!

_____

_____

## GOD'S RING

There are also times when a CHAMPION should not attempt to assume responsibility. Look at the outer ring of the Hoplon. This section of the shield represents God's Ring.

6. Read Psalm 28:7-8. Where does the strength of a CHAMPION come from?

_____

_____

7. Read John 15:4-5. What do you think it means to abide (some Bible translations say "remain") in Christ?

_____

_____

_____

8. What can we accomplish if we don't abide in Christ?

_____

_____

_____

_____

A CHAMPION takes responsibility for his actions, but everything else in life is God's responsibility and remains in God's Ring. If we obey God and seek Him daily, He will take care of us in every way.

9. Read Joshua 1:9. Why should we be strong and courageous?

_____

_____

_____

10. Name one thing that you worry about, something you currently keep in the CHAMPION's Ring that really should be placed into God's Ring.

_____

_____

_____

_____

_____

God's Ring encircles the CHAMPION's Ring because God is constantly with us, and His love surrounds us wherever we are. It is God's responsibility to watch over us and protect us. In fact, the Bible tells us that God is our shield (Psalm 28:7).

God is even responsible for paying for our failures and sins. Only He can give us eternal life through His Son, Jesus Christ. When we receive Jesus into our lives, we are given a special relationship as a son in God's family and covered by the protection of His all-powerful love.

If you don't yet have this kind of personal relationship with God, but would like to be under His love and protection, turn to the section entitled Just Do It! in the Appendix.

# The Main Things I learned in this Champion Session are:

_____

_____

_____

_____

_____

## CHAMPION
### Sheet of Deeds

Go to the CHAMPION Sheet of Deeds on page 9 and write down **one thing you will do** in the upcoming days (and beyond) to apply the main things you learned in session 1.

# Your Mission

Complete your mission and CHAMPION Session prep before you meet for session 2A.

## Power Verse: Philippians 4:6-7

**Date memorized:** _____

## Critical Maneuver

This will reinforce what you learned today. Obtain your maneuver instructions from your father.

## CHAMPION Sheet of Deeds

Begin to apply your action point from your Sheet of Deeds.

## CHAMPION Session Prep

Reread episode 2 of *Teknon and the CHAMPION Warriors*, and then complete the questions in session 2A of your *Mission Guide* on your own. **Our next CHAMPION Session will be:**

Date: _____

Time: _____

Place: _____

# Session 2A:
# My Enemy, Your Enemy

## CHAMPION Characteristics
### Mental Toughness and Navigation

### Power Verse: James 4:7-8A

*Submit therefore to God. Resist the devil and he will flee from you.
Draw near to God and He will draw near to you.*

# Discussion Topics

**Assessing the enemy**
**Embracing the mission you have been given**
**Learning to defeat the enemy**

# Mission Debrief

1. Discuss your mission from session 1. Did you complete your maneuver? If so, what did you learn? If not, why not?

2. Did you start applying your first action point from your Sheet of Deeds? If so, what did you learn? Have you had any struggles in trying to apply it?

3. Recite your memory verse (Philippians 4:6-7) from session 1.

4. Read the CHAMPION Warrior Creed out loud together again (see page 5).

# Reconnaissance

1. Carefully review the Map of the Mission on page 8 before beginning this section. Identify where the team is located in episode 2.

2. What is the CHAMPION definition of **Mental Toughness**? Of **Navigation**? (Refer to the CHAMPION Code on page 6.)

_____

_____

_____

_____

3. In this episode, Kratos describes the team's primary enemy. Who is he and why is he so dangerous? What is he trying to do?

_____

_____

_____

_____

4. Who is the team's secondary enemy created by Magos? What is his function?

_____

_____

_____

_____

5. Why does Magos want to defeat Kratos?

_____

_____

6. What did Magos steal?  Why did he steal it?  Why did Kratos want to get it back?

_____

_____

7. Why did Kratos refuse to be recreated and join Magos?

_____

_____

8. What did Kratos mean when he said, "Where there is no character, there is no threat to Magos."

_____

_____

9. The Greek word *artios*, refers to something that is complete and fitted perfectly.   What does Artios (Arti) do to live up to his name?

_____

_____

_____

_____

# Strategy and Tactics

## Enemy Assessment

A hunter in the wilderness aimed at a bear with his gun. Suddenly the bear shouted, "Why do you want to shoot me?"

The hunter replied, "I need a fur coat for the winter."

The bear responded, "Well, all I want is a good breakfast. Why don't we sit down and discuss our needs?"

The hunter thought for a minute, then sat down and discussed the issue with the bear. After a short time, the only one left was the bear, who did indeed enjoy a good breakfast. The hunter ended up with a fur coat, but not at all in the way he had planned. In other words, the hunter let his guard down at the wrong time.

In the same way, Kratos knew he could not join Magos, or even discuss joining him. Kratos hated everything that his former partner wanted to accomplish. To join Magos, Kratos would have had to become like the cyborg, almost a part of the enemy he sought to defeat. Kratos realized he could not let his guard down for a minute with his enemy.

## Who Is Your Enemy?

Did you know that the Bible says you have an enemy? And did you realize that you should hate this enemy and everything that he stands for? Your enemy is Satan, also known as the devil. At one time, Satan was an angel, part of God's heavenly host (Isaiah 14:12-15, Luke 11:14-23).

But Satan became prideful and actually challenged God's authority. Like Magos, who chose to transform himself, Satan took matters into his own hands and allowed his pride to direct his actions. He wanted to become something he was not. He wanted to become God. As a result, God kicked him out of heaven forever.

When Satan was cast out, many of the other angels joined him in his rebellion. These angels now serve him around the world, which is currently in his control (1 John 5:19), by tempting, seducing, and enticing us to disobey God. Just like Scandalon is serving Magos, these angels serve Satan in his evil schemes.

Satan hates you and everything about you because he hates God. If you have invited Christ into your life, you are going to spend eternity with Christ in heaven. That is something Satan will never be able to do. Satan's mission is to ruin as many people as he can. He wants to accomplish his mission before Christ comes back again to rule forever.

1. Read 1 Peter 5:8. What does the Bible say that Satan wants to do to us?

_____

_____

_____

2. How should we respond to Satan's plan for us?

_____

_____

_____

_____

_____

_____

_____

Satan wants to infect our thoughts, our desires, and our actions so that we will be ineffective for God. If you are a Christian, Satan can't prevent you from going to heaven, but he can make your life ineffective and miserable if you allow him to do so. What's worse, he will use your poor choices, ineffectiveness, and disobedience to display you as a poor example of God's sons to the world.

3. What do you think Satan would like for us to think about?

_____

_____

Remember, Satan is a brilliant enemy (see Ephesians 6:10-18). Never underestimate him. He knows what tempts you and then plots to bring those temptations into your path. Every time you make a decision in obedience to God, Satan loses. Every time you make a wrong decision, like telling a lie or cheating on a test, he leaves you to deal with the consequences and brings a more serious temptation into your path, hoping you will make the wrong decision again.

But there's good news! God knows that Satan is your enemy. Your Heavenly Father wants to provide all of the strength you need to defeat Satan every day. Through Jesus' death, burial, and resurrection, He has defeated the devil (Genesis 3:15) and has overcome the world (John 16:33). All you have to do is put your trust in Christ and obey His instructions to be victorious.

## DEFEATING THE ENEMY

4. Read James 4:7-8. What does the Bible say to do to the devil to make him flee from you?

_____

_____

_____

*My message to you is: Be courageous! ... Be as brave as your fathers before you. Have faith! Go forward.*

Thomas A. Edison

5. Why is it important for us to admit that Satan has influence in this world?

_____

_____

6. Should we fear Satan?  Why or why not?

_____

_____

_____

The Bible also says, "Greater is He [Christ] who is in you than he who is in the world [Satan]."  You must realize that Satan is a formidable enemy, but you do not need to fear him.  If you are a Christian, you belong to Almighty God, so He will give you guidance and protection.  God also assigns His angels to us; they are charged with guarding those who fear and follow Him (Psalm 34:7, 91:11).

7. What can you do to protect yourself according to God's instructions in Psalm 119:9-11?

_____

_____

_____

_____

_____

_____

_____

_____

*"Have I not commanded you? Be strong and courageous! Do not tremble or be dismayed, for the Lord your God is with you wherever you go."*

Joshua 1:9

## The Main Things I learned
## in this Champion Session are:

_____

_____

_____

_____

_____

## CHAMPION
### SHEET OF DEEDS

Go to the CHAMPION Sheet of Deeds on page 9 and write down **one thing you will begin to do** before the next session (and beyond) to apply the main things you learned in session 2A.

# Your Mission

Complete your mission and CHAMPION Session Prep before you meet for session 2B.

## POWER VERSE: JAMES 4:7–8A

**Date memorized:** _____

## CRITICAL MANEUVER

This will reinforce what you learned today. Obtain your maneuver instructions from your father.

## CHAMPION SHEET OF DEEDS

Begin to apply your action point from your Sheet of Deeds.

## CHAMPION SESSION PREP

Reread episode 2 of *Teknon and the CHAMPION Warriors*, and then complete the questions in session 2B in your *Mission Guide* on your own. **Our next CHAMPION Session will be:**

DATE: _____

TIME: _____

PLACE: _____

# Session 2B:
# My Enemy, Your Enemy

## Champion Characteristic

### Ownership

## Power Verse: Luke 16:10 (NIV)

*Whoever can be trusted with very little can also be trusted with much, and whoever is dishonest with very little will also be dishonest with much.*

# Discussion Topics

### Learning that God owns all things
### Becoming an effective steward of our resources

# Mission Debrief

1. Discuss your mission from session 2A. Did you complete your maneuver? If so, what did you learn? If not, why not?

2. Did you start applying your new action point from your Sheet of Deeds? How are these action points affecting your mind-set?

3. Recite your power verse (James 4:7-8a) from session 2B.

4. Read the CHAMPION Warrior Creed out loud together again (see page 5).

# Reconnaissance

1. Carefully review the Map of the Mission on page 8 before beginning this section. Identify where the team is located in episode 2.

2. What is the CHAMPION definition of **Ownership**? (Refer to the CHAMPION Code on page 6.)

_____

_____

_____

_____

3. Why did Teknon buy the Shocktech?

_____

_____

_____

4. Did Teknon need the Shocktech? Why or why not?

_____

_____

_____

5a. Was Teknon free to spend his money the way he chose to spend it?

_____

_____

_____

_____

5b. Was Teknon wise in the spending choice he made?  Why?

_____

_____

6. What did Kratos recommend to Teknon about spending money?

_____

_____

_____

_____

7. What do you think is the difference between a need and a want?

_____

_____

_____

8. Kratos said, "You can splurge once in a while, but give yourself enough time to think about it before you make the purchase."  What items are you tempted to buy impulsively?

_____

_____

_____

# STRATEGY AND TACTICS

## EFFECTIVE STEWARDSHIP

1. Is it wrong to spend money?  Absolutely not, but God wants us to spend it wisely.  Did you know there are more verses in the Bible concerning money than on almost any other subject?  Why do you think there are so many verses about money?

_____

_____

Money is a tool God has given each of us to use and to manage.  The way you manage money often reflects what you think about Who provided it to you.  Managing money is a visible expression of your relationship with God—your values and your trust in Him.

2. What can happen when a family gets into the habit of spending money on the spur of the moment like Teknon did?

_____

_____

3. Ecclesiastes was written by King Solomon, one of the richest people who ever lived.  Solomon had more money than he could spend, although the Bible says he spent quite a bit.  What does Ecclesiastes 2:10-11 say about spending money?

_____

_____

_____

Solomon realized that he shouldn't have been so frivolous and irresponsible in his spending. Likewise, whether you have a lot of money or a little money, God expects you to use it wisely. When you do that, you are considered a good steward or manager.

4. According to Matthew 25:14-30, how much money did the owner give each servant? How did he decide what to give each one?

_____

_____

_____

5. What did the owner want the servants to do with the money?

_____

_____

_____

6. Which servants were good stewards?

_____

_____

_____

7. What do you think is the difference between an owner and a steward?

_____

_____

_____

God is the owner of all good and perfect things on this earth. We are His stewards. What a privilege we have to be entrusted by God with His resources! God doesn't mind if you spend money. He may not even mind if you occasionally spend money on something you really want that you really don't need. But that should be the exception, not the rule.

Remember, God owns it all—our time, our talent, our possessions, and our money. He entrusts them to us. Think about what you buy before you buy it. Don't buy on the spur of the moment. Think and pray for wisdom before you make a big purchase. Seek wise counsel from others who are good stewards.

8. How can you become a good steward of your money and possessions?

_____

_____

_____

_____

_____

Be a good steward of everything that God entrusts to you. And remember, never spend more than 100 specas for a Shocktech!

## The Main Things I learned in this Champion Session are:

_____

_____

_____

_____

_____

_____

## CHAMPION
### SHEET OF DEEDS

Go to the CHAMPION Sheet of Deeds on page 9 and write down **one thing you will begin to do** before the next session (and beyond) to apply the main things you learned in session 2B.

# YOUR MISSION

Complete your mission and CHAMPION Session Prep before you meet for session 3.

## POWER VERSE:  LUKE 16:10

Date memorized: _____

## CRITICAL MANEUVER

This will reinforce what you learned today.  Obtain your maneuver instructions from your father.

## CHAMPION SHEET OF DEEDS

Begin to apply your action point from your Sheet of Deeds.

## — CHAMPION SESSION PREP —

Reread episode 3 of *Teknon and the CHAMPION Warriors*, and then complete the questions in session 3 in your *Mission Guide* on your own.  **Our next CHAMPION Session will be:**

DATE: _____

TIME: _____

PLACE: _____

COURAGE • HONOR • ATTITUDE • MENTAL TOUGHNESS • PURITY • INTEGRITY • OWNERSHIP • NAVIGATION

# SESSION 3:
# THE SECOND LOOK

### CHAMPION Characteristic

**Purity**

### POWER VERSE: 1 CORINTHIANS 6:18

*Flee immorality. Every other sin that a man commits is outside the body, but the immoral man sins against his own body.*

# Discussion Topics

**Understanding the right context for sex**
**Establishing boundaries in physical intimacy**
**Setting high standards to guard your purity**

1. Discuss your mission from session 2B. What did you learn from your maneuver? How is what you've learned affecting your thinking or behavior?

   _____

   _____

2. Did you start applying your new action point from your Sheet of Deeds? Any progress to report? Any struggles?

   _____

   _____

3. Recite your power verse (Luke 16:10) from session 2B.

4. What are a few things that God has entrusted to you (for example: money, talents, time) that require good steward-ship? How will you be a faithful steward?

   _____

   _____

5. Recite as much as you can of the CHAMPION Warrior Creed from memory (see page 5).

# RECONNAISSANCE

1. Review the Map of the Mission on page 8 and determine the team's location in episode 3.

2. What is the CHAMPION definition of **Purity**? (Refer to the CHAMPION Code on page 6.)

_____

_____

_____

3. Why do you think Scandalon tempted Teknon?

_____

_____

_____

4. When should Teknon have returned to camp? Why?

_____

_____

_____

_____

5. What did Teknon mean when he said, "I guess I shouldn't have taken the second look"?

_____

_____

_____

6a. What did Kratos mean when he said, "Error increases with distance"?

_____

_____

_____

6b. How does that insight relate to physical and sexual intimacy?

_____

_____

7. What point did Kratos want to make by mentioning the story of the transtron racer and the cliff?

_____

_____

_____

_____

8. Why do you think Kratos suggested that Teknon wait until marriage to kiss a woman?

_____

_____

_____

9. How did Teknon react to the idea of the Wedding Kiss?

_____

_____

## Optional Questions

10. Kratos said, "If a couple will wait to experience sex in the correct setting of marriage, they will receive incredible benefits of trust, bonding, and sheer enjoyment. However, if sex is misused, many long-term problems can occur." What kind of problems is he talking about?

_____

_____

11. What do you think Kratos meant when he said, "Once you take a step closer to the edge [physical intimacy], it's very difficult to take a step back"?

_____

_____

_____

45

# Strategy and Tactics

## Right Time, Right Place, Right Person

*While leading a discussion on the topic of sexual purity with a class of engaged couples, the teacher explored the importance of waiting until marriage to have sexual intimacy. He brought out a small, bright, delicate metal object and asked, "What do you think this is?"*

*"A small pair of pliers," someone replied.*

*"Actually," the teacher said, "this is a $500 pair of fishhook removers." He held the tool in the air and pretended that he was removing a hook from a fish's mouth. "If you reach way down into the fish's mouth, you can remove the hook without damaging the fish."*

*The couples were quite impressed, but then another person asked, "Why in the world would anyone pay that much money for a fishhook remover?"*

*"My point exactly. Why would anyone pay that much to remove a hook from a fish's mouth?" the teacher responded. "Actually, this isn't really a fishhook remover. It's a delicate 'needle holder' used in brain surgery to hold a suture. This tool holds a suture so fine that it's hardly visible to the human eye. The neurosurgeon uses this surgical instrument under a powerful microscope during surgery. This instrument is so carefully balanced that it doesn't make the surgeon's hand tired when he sews brain tissue for long periods of time. And because of its special design and its $500 price tag, the instrument is handled carefully throughout the hospital. When used in the proper environment—the operating room—it's a wonderful tool.*

*"Now," the teacher continued, "can this valuable surgical instrument be used as a fishhook remover?"*

*"Yes," the couples answered.*

*"Is a tackle box the environment for which this finely crafted instrument was made?" the teacher asked.*

*"No!" the couples exclaimed.*

*"Likewise," the teacher went on, "God created sex for a*

*special environment—marriage. Whenever we take sex out of the environment for which it was created, it becomes tainted and corroded, just like this fine surgical instrument would be if it were tossed into a tackle box."*

As this story illustrates, sex is wonderful. God designed it that way. The book in the Bible called the Song of Solomon reveals the physical love between a husband and wife and the beauty of their sexual relationship. God designed sex to be the ultimate physical closeness that a man and his wife can experience. No wonder it's difficult to keep our minds from becoming consumed with the subject of sex! It is something to look forward to, but to experience all of the blessings God has for you in a marriage relationship, you must wait for His perfect timing. God's plan for some men is that they do not marry so that they can be set apart in a special way as a single man in His service. But for most of us, God already has a special woman picked out to be our bride and partner for life.

1. Read 2 Corinthians 10:3-5. How can we win the battle for purity in our minds and hearts?

_____

_____

_____

2a. Read Romans 6:12-13. What does God say we should not do with our bodies?

_____

_____

2b. What does He say we should do with our bodies?

_____

_____

_____

Just as Scandalon tempted Teknon, your enemy—Satan—wants to tempt you to fail in the area of sexual purity. If he can destroy your character, you are no longer a threat to him. Satan often uses sex to tempt us to sin. He sets traps for us and, if we don't allow God to control our desires, we'll walk right into them.

3. What does the Bible say about temptation in 1 Corinthians 10:13? How much can we depend on God when we are tempted?

_____

_____

God promises to provide a way out during any temptation we face. It may mean that we shouldn't take the second look. It will probably mean getting out of the tempting situation as quickly as possible. Remember, God promises to provide the power for you to live a pure life.

## THE WEDDING KISS

Now, think about the Wedding Kiss. It's a pretty radical idea, right? But why not take every precaution possible to make sure that you will have the most fulfilling and intimate life possible with the wife God may eventually bring into your life? The world's approach to sex is not about creating more exciting and satisfying relationships, although the movie and music industry would try to tell us otherwise. Sure the Wedding Kiss challenge sounds weird in today's society, but it's worth waiting for the benefits you'll receive in the long run. Besides, God is the one who designed sex; let's try it His way! Kratos said that he wished someone had challenged him to meet such a goal. There are probably many men today who wish they had received a challenge like this when they were your age.

4a. Read 1 Thessalonians 4:1-5. How do the Gentiles (non-Christians) behave regarding sexual activity?

_____

_____

**4b.** How does God say He wants you to behave in this area?

_____

The idea of the Wedding Kiss is not just a trendy fad to consider for a while and then move on to something else. It is a brave and bold commitment to purity. It's holding on to the precious gift of your body and emotions until you can give that gift to one special person. People who choose to refrain from sexual intimacy before marriage will be blessed by God in powerful ways.

5. What do you think your friends would think about the idea of the Wedding Kiss? How far do you think most teens will go physically with a girl?

_____

_____

6. Whether you go for the Wedding Kiss or not, you need to decide in advance how far you will go emotionally and physically with a girl before you are married. Have you ever really thought about how far you plan to go?

_____

You may have already taken a few steps toward the cliff that Kratos talked about. You may have kissed a girl, or maybe become even more physically and emotionally involved with her. If you have, now is the time to confess this to God and seek His forgiveness. Then, recommit yourself to a higher standard. Claim God's promise of forgiveness and cleansing (1 John 1:9), and start fresh today in this area of purity.

---

## Optional Question

7. What would you have said and done if you were Teknon when Lana surprised him behind the bushes?

_____

## The Main Things I learned in this Champion Session are:

_____

_____

_____

_____

_____

*Walk by the Spirit,
and you will not
carry out the desire
of the flesh.*

Galatians 5:16b

## CHAMPION
### SHEET OF DEEDS

Go to the CHAMPION Sheet of
Deeds on page 9 and write down **one
thing you will begin to do** before
the next session (and beyond) to
apply the main things you learned
in session 3.

# Your Mission

Complete your mission and CHAMPION Session prep before you meet for session 4.

## Power Verse: 1 Corinthians 6:18

**Date memorized:** _____

## Critical Maneuver

This will reinforce what you learned in this session. Obtain your maneuver instructions from your father.

## CHAMPION Sheet of Deeds

Begin to apply your action point from your Sheet of Deeds.

## —— CHAMPION Session Prep ——

Reread episode 4 of *Teknon and the CHAMPION Warriors*, and then complete the questions in session 4 in your *Mission Guide* on your own. **Our next CHAMPION Session will be:**

DATE:

_____

TIME:

_____

PLACE:

_____

# SESSION 4:
# THE COMPANY I KEEP

CHAMPION Characteristics
## Mental Toughness and Integrity

POWER VERSE: 1 CORINTHIANS 15:33

*Do not be misled: "Bad company corrupts good character." (NIV)*

# Discussion Topics

**Recognizing the importance of discernment in choosing friends**
**Realizing that there are always consequences to our choices**
**Recovering from failures—part 1**

# Mission Debrief

1.  Discuss your mission from session 3. Are you taking the responsibility to complete and learn from your critical maneuvers?

    _____

2.  Are you continuing to apply your action points from the Sheet of Deeds? If so, how is it going? If not, what would help you to start applying your action points?

    _____

3.  Recite your power verse (1 Corinthians 6:18) from session 3.

4.  Are you struggling with any sexual desires that could lead to temptation? If so, what can you do to deal with those desires (the CHAMPION's Ring)? What strength and protection do you need to gain from the Lord (God's Ring)?

    _____

    _____

5.  Try to recite at least half of the CHAMPION Warrior Creed from memory (see page 5).

    _____

    _____

# RECONNAISSANCE

1. Review the Map of the Mission on page 8 and determine the team's location in episode 4.

2. What is the CHAMPION definition of **Mental Toughness**? Of **Integrity**? (Refer to the CHAMPION Code on page 6.)

_____

_____

_____

_____

_____

*It's not whether you get knocked down, it's whether you get up.*

Vince Lombardi

3a. Do you believe Teknon used good judgment in Bia? Why or why not?

_____

_____

3b. If not, at which moments in this episode did he show a lack of discernment?

_____

_____

_____

4. When should Teknon have realized that he should avoid the Harpax?

_____

_____

5. The leader of the Harpax is named Rhegma. The Greek word *rhegma* means "ruin." In what ways could a person like Rhegma ruin the life of a young man who would join the Harpax group

_____

_____

_____

There's a story about a zoo that had a lion pavilion. One day, a visitor to the zoo was astonished as he looked in the lion cage and saw a lamb and a lion lying down together. The man couldn't believe that the natural enemies lived so peacefully together. He grabbed the zookeeper by the arm and asked him how such a wonderful relationship could occur. The zookeeper replied, "It's easy, Mister, we just add fresh lambs now and then."

When you make friends with the wrong people, like Teknon did with the Harpax, you can end up in trouble. Bottom line: be careful whom you trust and to whom you offer friendship.

## Optional Question

6. Why do you think Kratos allowed Teknon to meet with the Harpax?

_____

_____

7. What did Kratos mean when he said, "It's better to be trusted and respected than it is to be liked"?

_____

_____

8. Kratos also told Teknon that he must learn from his mistake and to recover. What does it mean to recover? How would you recover if you made a mistake like Teknon made?

_____

_____

---

## ОРТІΟΠAL QUESTIONS

9. Kratos cautioned, "Observe all of the characteristics of a person." What characteristics should you watch for?

GOOD Characteristics:

_____

_____

BAD Characteristics:

_____

_____

10. What do you think Kratos meant when he said, "Bad humor is a sign of bad morals"?

_____

_____

*Hold yourself responsible for a higher standard than anybody else expects of you. Never excuse yourself.*

Henry Ward Beecher

# STRATEGY AND TACTICS

We need friends that not only make us feel good, but also cause us to do good things.  Because of this, it is important to seek God's wisdom as you develop friendships.

Most of the book of Proverbs in the Old Testament was written by one of the wisest men who ever lived, King Solomon.  In this book, Solomon instructed his sons and the young men of his kingdom about the difference between knowledge (having the facts) and wisdom (applying those facts to life).  Like Teknon, young men can choose to reject the wisdom of their parents and the Word of God.  As they grow older, however, they will increase their knowledge, but not their wisdom and discernment.  In Proverbs 1, Solomon described the danger of being a young man who lacks discernment.

1a. Read Proverbs 1.  What can a person do to begin obtaining wisdom?  (See verses 7-9.)

_____

*Rather fail with honor than succeed by fraud.*

Sophocles

1b. What advice did Solomon give in verses 15 and 16 concerning the importance of choosing the right friends?

_____

_____

1c. According to verses 23-27, why should we listen to sound advice and wisdom?

_____

1d. What will happen if we don't obey God and use discernment? (See verses 28-32.)

_____

_____

1e. What will happen if we use good judgment and listen to wisdom? (See verse 33.)

_____

Always remember two things about your Heavenly Father: God loves you and He is trustworthy.

## God loves you

Just as Kratos loved Teknon despite his bad decisions, so your Father in heaven loves you no matter what you do. He understands that you are growing and learning how to follow Him. Sometimes you will succeed, and sometimes you will fail. As you grow to know Him better and seek to obey His Word, you will increase in discernment and find it easier to make better choices.

But no matter how hard we try, we will still sin and disobey God. Romans 3:23 tells us that we have all sinned. God understands us and loves us so much that He sent Jesus to die on the cross and then raised Him again from the dead to pay for our sins (or failures). After we sin, we recover by confessing our failure to God and then claiming His promise of forgiveness. Then, we turn from our own way and go God's way. We should also apologize to anyone we have offended.

2. What does 1 John 1:9 say about God and confessing our sins to Him? How does this make you feel?

_____

_____

## God is trustworthy

God is trustworthy and all-knowing. If you need wisdom, you can trust Him to provide it for you. All you have to do is ask.

"If you want to know what God wants you to do, ask Him, and He will gladly tell you, for He is always ready to give a bountiful supply of wisdom to all who ask Him; He will not resent it." (James 1:5 TLB)

*Associate yourself with men of good quality if you esteem your own reputation; for it is better to be alone than in bad company.*

George Washington

3. In what ways can God give you answers about choosing friends and other issues?

_____

_____

4. Why is belief in who God is so important?

_____

As a future CHAMPION, you must remember to ask for wisdom before you enter situations like those Teknon faced in the city of Bia.  In other words, use good judgment ahead of time and study how God wants you to respond before you enter a tempting situation.

---

## Optional Questions

5. Kratos used the Hoplon to become invisible.  What would you do if you could become invisible?

_____

6. What kind of friend will help you to do good as well as to feel good?  What are the characteristics of such a person?

_____

7. Why did George Washington say, "It's better to be alone than in bad company"?

_____

_____

_____

---

## The Main Things I learned in this Champion Session are:

_____

_____

_____

_____

_____

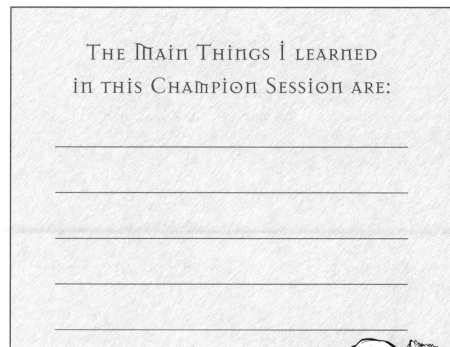

## CHAMPION
### Sheet of Deeds

Go to the CHAMPION Sheet of Deeds on page 9 and write down **one thing you will begin to do in** before the next session (and beyond) to apply the main things you learned in session 4.

Complete your mission and CHAMPION Session prep before you meet for Session 5.

## POWER VERSE: 1 CORINTHIANS 15:33

**Date memorized:** _____

## CRITICAL MANEUVER

This will reinforce what you learned today. Obtain your maneuver instructions from your father.

## CHAMPION SHEET OF DEEDS

Begin to apply your action point from your Sheet of Deeds.

## —— CHAMPION SESSION PREP ——

Reread episode 5 of *Teknon and the CHAMPION Warriors*, and then complete the questions in session 5 in your *Mission Guide* on your own. **Our next CHAMPION Session will be:**

*He who walks with wise men will be wise, but the companion of fools will suffer harm.*

Proverbs 13:20

DATE:

TIME:

PLACE:

COURAGE • HONOR • ATTITUDE • MENTAL TOUGHNESS • PURITY • INTEGRITY • OWNERSHIP • NAVIGATION

# SESSION 5:
# ERGONIAN PRIDE

## CHAMPION Characteristc

**Attitude**

POWER VERSE: PROVERBS 19:20 (NIV)

*Listen to advice and accept instruction, and in the end
you will be wise.*

# Discussion Topics

### Uncovering the danger of pride
### Learning the importance of a teachable attitude
### Listening to wise counsel

# Mission Debrief

1.  Discuss your mission from session 4. What did you learn from your maneuver? How is what you learned affecting your thinking or behavior?

    _____

    _____

    _____

2.  Did you start applying your new action point from the Sheet of Deeds? If so, how is it going?

    _____

    _____

    _____

3.  Recite your power verse (1 Corinthians 15:33) from session 4.

4a. If you are spending time with people who influence you in bad ways, what steps should you take to change that situation? (Remember, the CHAMPION's Ring from session 1 contains those areas that you can and should control.)

    _____

    _____

4b. Are you are worried about any other people's perception of you? Is it difficult for you to trust God with those perceptions and your concerns? If so, why do you think that is? (This is part of God's Ring, the area that only He can control and that we need to release to Him.)

_____

_____

5. Try to recite all of the CHAMPION Warrior Creed from memory (see page 5).

# RECONNAISSANCE

1. Review the Map of the Mission on page 8 and determine the team's location in episode 5. Trace the steps the team has covered thus far, reviewing story highlights and main topics discussed.

_____

_____

_____

2. What is the CHAMPION definition of **Attitude**? (Refer to the CHAMPION Code on page 6.)

_____

_____

_____

_____

3. What kind of attitude did Mr. Poroo have toward Kratos? Why?

_____

_____

4. Why did Kratos say, "That attitude might be his undoing"?

_____

_____

5. What occurred as a result of Mr. Poroo's attitude?

_____

_____

6. In what ways might Mr. Poroo have responded differently to Kratos' suggestion? How would the outcome have been different ?

_____

_____

7. What does the word "teachability" mean to you? Be specific!

_____

_____

Gleukos was the socially acceptable intoxicant consumed by the resort guests at Ergo. Kratos explained why the guests used this substance: "This is a place to escape. For a few days, all these people want to do is to forget about their lives at home. Sun, fun, eating, and drinking gleukos is what this place is all about."

8. What do you think about teens drinking alcohol? What about adults?

---

# Strategy and Tactics

## Easy Mistakes

Have you ever acted like you knew it all? We all have. Let's say you're facing an important decision, like buying a new sound system. You see one you like, but don't really know how good it is. You know your neighbor is an expert on these systems and could provide you with excellent information to help you decide which one to buy and might even know the best place to buy it. But you have your pride and don't want to reveal your lack of "surround sound, high density, bass-enriched" expertise. So you don't ask anyone for advice, especially your expert neighbor. What do you do? You buy an overpriced player that breaks down within three months. Of course, the warranty is only good for 30 days.

A few days later, you're over at a new friend's house on a rainy day. Your friend is a proud owner of a new, streamlined dirt bike. He tells you there's no better time to dirt bike than on a rainy day; in fact, the wetter the better. He tells you that if you haven't ridden a dirt bike before, he'd be more than happy to give you a quick lesson. You've never ridden anything more tenacious than a 10-speed, but that's a well-kept secret. *Nothing doing*, you say to yourself. You're not about to look "mechanically challenged" around your buddy. What do you do? You jump on, rev the engine and pop the clutch. Thirty feet of mud and a compound fracture later, you're wondering why you didn't take your friend up on his free introductory lesson.

After you get out of the hospital, your dad expresses concern about one of your new friends. He's bothered that this new acquaintance encourages you to watch dirty movies, tell lies, and use vulgar language. You immediately respond by defending the friend and declaring that your dad is intolerant and that he's overreacting. Basically you ignore the whole discussion. A couple months later, you're using profanity, struggling with pornography, and lying to your parents to cover it up.

*Life would be much easier if we were teachable, wouldn't it?*

1. What does Proverbs 19:20 say about being teachable?

_____

2. What happens if you are not teachable? (Read Proverbs 29:1.)

_____

_____

Read Proverbs 16:18-19 and Proverbs 18:12.

3a. What kind of attitude creates the greatest barrier to becoming teachable and leads to your destruction in the end?

_____

3b. What kind of attitude makes us teachable and leads to honor?

_____

_____

4. According to Psalm 50:15, who should we call on first if we need help or have a big decision to make? How will He respond?

_____

_____

If you have invited Jesus into your life as your Savior and Lord, you are a child of God. God loves it when His children call on Him. When we seek God, we honor Him. Jeremiah 29:11-13 (TLB) says, "For I know the plans I have for you," says the Lord. "They are plans for good and not for evil, to give you a future and a hope. In those days when you pray, I will listen. You will find me when you seek me if you look for me in earnest."

God knows what is best for us. When we reject God's wisdom and direction in our decisions, we are trying to do His job. When we aren't teachable, we don't pay attention to God's Word. We also don't listen to people whom God puts into our lives to give us advice and counsel—like our parents, pastors, and teachers. We saw what happened to Mr. Poroo when he didn't listen to Kratos' advice. Make sure you are seeking God with a teachable heart so that He can reveal how to live your life for Him.

5. Do you think your friends (name a few) are teachable? Why or why not?

Read Proverbs 6:20-23

*My son, observe the commandment of your father and do not forsake the teaching of your mother; bind them continually on your heart; tie them around your neck. When you walk about, they will guide you; when you sleep, they will watch over you; and when you awake, they will talk to you. For the commandment is a lamp, and the teaching is light; and reproofs for discipline are the way of life ... .*

_____

_____

6a. What are the some of the benefits of listening to your parents?

_____

6b. Has this discussion changed your view about the importance of your parents' advice and discipline? How so? Do you need to adjust your attitude in this area?

_____

_____

*Success isn't forever, and failure isn't fatal.*

Don Shula

# The Main Things I learned in this Champion Session are:

_____

_____

_____

_____

*Teachability is a man's capacity for growth.*

Howard Hendricks

## CHAMPION
### SHEET OF DEEDS

Go to the **CHAMPION** Sheet of Deeds on page 9 and write down **one thing you will begin to do** before the next session (and beyond) to apply the main things you learned in session 5.

# Your Mission

Complete your mission and CHAMPION Session Prep before you meet for session 6.

## Power Verse: Proverbs 19:20

Date memorized: _____

## Critical Maneuver

This will reinforce what you learned in this session. Obtain your maneuver instructions from your father.

## CHAMPION Sheet of Deeds

Begin to apply your action point from your Sheet of Deeds.

## — CHAMPION Session Prep —

Reread episode 6 of Teknon and the CHAMPION Warriors, and then complete the questions in session 6 in your Mission Guide on your own. **Our next CHAMPION Session will be:**

Date:

Time:

Place:

*Spend less time worrying who's right, and spend more time deciding what's right!*

*Life's Little Instruction Book*

# Session 6:
# A Storm of Dishonor

## CHAMPION Characteristics
### Honor and Attitude

Power Verse: Romans 12:10

*Be devoted to one another in brotherly love; give preference to one another in honor.*

# Discussion Topics

**Showing respect to family members**

**Showing honor—placing value on people and communicating that value to them**

# Mission Debrief

1. Discuss your mission from session 5. What did you learn from your maneuver? How is what you've learned affecting your thinking and behavior?

   _____

   _____

2. Did you start applying your new action point from the Sheet of Deeds? If so, what are you learning? If not, what would help you to get started?

   _____

   _____

3. Recite your power verse (Proverbs 19:20) from session 5.

4. Think about any area(s) of your life in which you need to be more teachable. What are they? What will you change to become more teachable? (Attitudes and actions like these, which you control, are within the CHAMPION's Ring.)

   _____

   _____

5. Try to recite all of the CHAMPION Warrior Creed from memory (see page 5). Say it slowly and think about which characteristics mean the most to you.

# RECONNAISSANCE

1. Review the Map of the Mission on page 8 and determine the team's location in episode 6.

2. What is the CHAMPION definition of **Honor**? Of **Attitude**? (Refer to the CHAMPION Code on page 6.)

_____

_____

_____

_____

3. How did Pikros and Parakoe treat their father? What did they reveal about their relationship with him?

_____

_____

4. How did Pikros and Parakoe treat each other?

_____

_____

_____

5. How did Teknon feel as he observed the boys' attitudes toward their father? Why did he feel this way?

_____

_____

## Optional Questions

6. In the Greek, *pikros* refers to acting bitterly. Pikros was disrespectful to his father and bitter about their relationship. Why do you think Pikros was bitter about the relationship with his father?

_____

7. Ameleo said, "I try to give them [my sons] everything they want." Why didn't this help Pikros and Parakoe to develop a better attitude toward their father? What did they really need and want?

_____

_____

_____

_____

*Kind words do not cost much ... yet they accomplish much.*

Blaise Pascal

8. What did Kratos mean when he said, "No matter what we accomplish or who we impress, if we don't treat our family and friends with respect, we have nothing to offer"?

_____

_____

_____

9. How did watching Pikros and Parakoe affect Teknon's attitude toward his sister Hilly?

_____

_____

_____

10. Do you think Teknon shows respect toward his father and mother?  Why do you think so?

_____

_____

_____

> *The deepest principle in human nature is the craving to be appreciated.*
>
> **William James**

# Strategy and Tactics

Honor and respect seem to be lost virtues in our society. We suffer from what has been called "a toxic atmosphere of cynicism" throughout the schools and boardrooms of our country.  A newspaper article entitled "Nasty as We Wanna Be" lamented our current attitudes by stating that:

> *The old values of courtesy, politeness, and respect have been trampled under.  We, as men, need to communicate to our sons what it means to show respect and esteem to the individuals God brings into our lives.  The indignities of the road are compounded with further indignities at work, at the movies, on the radio, from the profane mouths of strangers, and in battles between neighbors.  Pretty soon, you've got more than a headache. You've got a crisis on your hands.*
>
> *If we, as Christians, don't lead the way toward honoring people and treating them with dignity as individuals created by God, who will?[1]*

# An Honorable Attitude

Read Exodus 20:12. This is one of the Ten Commandments.

1a. What does this commandment say about the attitude young people should have toward their parents?

_____

1b. What does God promise the results will be if we obey His commandment?

_____

_____

2. What are some practical ways in which you can show honor to your parents? (Remember the CHAMPION's Ring involves your attitude and behavior.)

_____

_____

_____

3. What does Galatians 6:9-10 say about how young people should treat their brothers and sisters?

_____

_____

_____

_____

*Most of us, swimming against the tides of trouble the world knows nothing about, need only a bit of praise or encouragement— and we'll make the goal.*

Jerome P. Fleishman

4. Read Romans 12:10. How can we "do good" within our family?

_____

_____

_____

_____

The Bible says we ought to "do good to all people." That should especially apply to our family members.

5. How do you view your parents? How about your brothers and sisters? Do you act like Pikros and Parakoe? Or do you view your family, even with their flaws, as valuable people given to you by God?

_____

_____

The members of your family are valuable gifts that God has given you. Are they always easy to get along with? No way! Are you?

Does what they do always make sense? Absolutely not! Does what you do always make sense? Enough said.

A CHAMPION strives to maintain the right attitudes, no matter what other people do. Read Genesis 37:18-36. Joseph's brothers sold him into slavery because they were jealous of him. Even though his capture was a terrible thing, God used Joseph's captivity in an awesome way to eventually place Joseph as the second most powerful man in the Egyptian empire.

Read Genesis 45 to see how Joseph forgave his brothers even when he had the power to hurt them. Joseph understood that "God causes all things to work together for good to those who love God, to those who are called according to His purpose" (see Romans 8:28b).

6a. If your brother or sister doesn't show you honor, what should you do?

_____

_____

_____

6b. Why should you respond this way?

_____

_____

_____

You should honor your parents as God's chosen authority in your life. If you have any brothers and sisters, you should honor them as treasured co-workers and help your family to become all that God wants it to be. Don't end up like Pikros and Parakoe. Remember, you honor God by the way you treat other people. Take steps as a CHAMPION to maintain the right *Attitude* and show *Honor* to your family.

7. What are some practical ways you can you show honor to your mother? How about your brothers and sisters?

_____

_____

_____

# The Main Things I learned in this Champion Session are:

_____

_____

_____

_____

_____

*A man's wisdom gives him patience; it is to his glory to overlook an offense.*

Proverbs 19:11
(NIV)

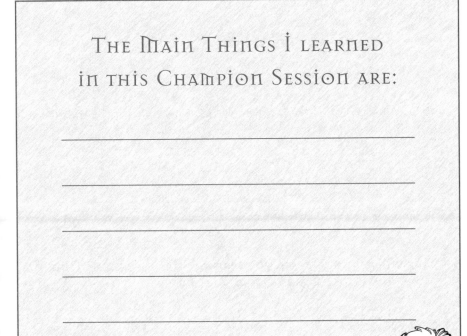

## CHAMPION
### Sheet of Deeds

Go to the CHAMPION Sheet of Deeds on page 9 and write down **one thing you will begin to do** before the next session (and beyond) to apply the main things you learned in session 6.

# Your Mission

Complete your mission and CHAMPION Session Prep before you meet for session 7.

## POWER VERSE: ROMANS 12:10

**Date memorized:** _____

## CRITICAL MANEUVER

This will reinforce what you learned in this session. Obtain your maneuver instructions from your father.

## CHAMPION SHEET OF DEEDS

Begin to apply your action point from your Sheet of Deeds.

## CHAMPION SESSION PREP

Reread episode 7 of *Teknon and the CHAMPION Warriors*, and then complete the questions in session 7 in your *Mission Guide* on your own. **Our next CHAMPION Session will be:**

DATE:

_____

TIME:

_____

PLACE:

_____

COURAGE • HONOR • ATTITUDE • MENTAL TOUGHNESS • PURITY • INTEGRITY • OWNERSHIP • NAVIGATION

# SESSION 7:
# AN EXCELLENT CHOICE

## CHAMPION Characteristics
### Purity and Integrity

POWER VERSE:  PSALM 101:3

*I will set no worthless thing before my eyes; I hate the work [deeds] of those who fall away; it shall not fasten its grip on me.*

# Discussion Topics

**Protecting your mind from inappropriate material**
**Avoiding temptation**
**Fleeing from temptation**
**Establishing your convictions in advance**

## Mission Debrief

1. Discuss your mission from session 6. What did you learn from your maneuver? How is this affecting your attitude or behavior?

   _____

   _____

2. Did you start applying your new action point from the Sheet of Deeds? What are some of the things you're learning from this and the previous action points?

   _____

   _____

3. Recite your power verse (Romans 12:10) from session 6.

4. Describe one situation when you honored your mother and/or father since the last CHAMPION Session? Describe one way you have honored your brothers/sisters or other family members? (Remember that honoring others is part of the actions and attitudes in the CHAMPION's Ring.)

   _____

   _____

5. Recite all of the CHAMPION Warrior Creed from memory (see page 5).

# RECONNAISSANCE

1. Review the Map of the Mission on page 8 before beginning this section. Identify where the team is located in episode 7.

2. Review the CHAMPION definition of **Purity** and of **Integrity** (refer to the CHAMPION Code on page 6.)

_____

_____

_____

_____

3. _Epios_ is a Greek word that refers to someone who shows patience and gentleness to other people. What does Epios (Epps) do to live up to his name?

_____

_____

_____

4. What did Eros try to get Teknon to do? Why?

_____

_____

_____

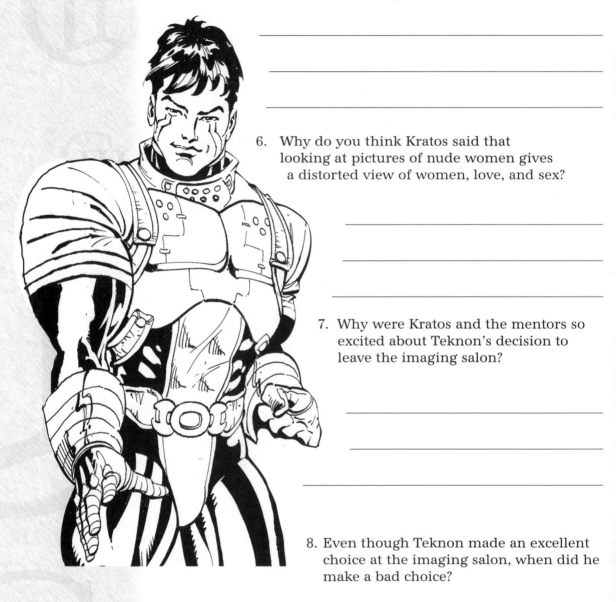

5. Why do you think Teknon chose not to stay in the image salon and look at the images?

_____

_____

_____

6. Why do you think Kratos said that looking at pictures of nude women gives a distorted view of women, love, and sex?

_____

_____

_____

7. Why were Kratos and the mentors so excited about Teknon's decision to leave the imaging salon?

_____

_____

_____

8. Even though Teknon made an excellent choice at the imaging salon, when did he make a bad choice?

_____

_____

_____

_____

Epps helped Teknon to see the danger that surrounded him when he said, "You [Teknon] took a big chance when you decided to go out on your own and walk past those places. All of us are tempted to look at bad material like that, but we can't afford to take those kinds of risks. We've got to stay as far away from them as possible."

# STRATEGY AND TACTICS

## DON'T PET THE T-REX!

Several years ago, my daughter and I went on a lunch date. After enjoying a great meal in the restaurant, we decided to walk through some nearby stores.

As soon as we entered a pet store named Fishes of the World, we knew that we had discovered a great place to explore. Exotic pets from around the world filled its cages and aquariums. We were surrounded by eels, fish, spiders, and snakes. One glass case was filled with very cute lizards—that's right cute lizards. They were about five inches long and had big, friendly eyes—almost like a Labrador Retriever. Just take my word for it: they were cute.

When the store's owner saw us pausing to look at the lizards, he took one out for us to hold. It snuggled in my hand and almost purred as my daughter and I petted it. "What's the name of this type of lizard? I asked.

"It's a Savannah Monitor," the owner said.

"Is this as big as it gets?" I asked, still petting the calm lizard.

"Oh, no," he responded. "In fact, there's a grown Savannah over there." We followed him around the corner to a much larger cage encased with thick wire. Inside was a reptile about four feet long that looked like it was on loan from the movie "Lost World." When my daughter and I stepped closer, the big lizard whipped around and snapped at the front of the cage.

"Yep," said the owner, "you can walk one around on a leash when it gets this size, but it'll drag you around a bit. You'd have to close in your backyard, of course." Then he added, "I wouldn't let children walk back there, though."

I found it hard to believe that the little, purring reptile I'd held in my hand a few minutes earlier could one day look at my children the way I look at a cheese pizza!

Bad habits are a lot like that cute little lizard. At first a bad habit seems harmless, and we don't believe there is any way it could hurt us. We get comfortable with it, feed it, and soon it begins to grow. Before long, it consumes more time and effort than before. In fact, the habit can become so strong that it is difficult to control. *Soon, it gets so powerful that it can start to control us and drag us around.*

Viewing pornography—sexually explicit material—is one of the most dangerous habits you can develop. It can be compared to petting a baby T-Rex and bringing it into your home. Why in the world would you want to pet a T-Rex *or* bring it into your home? You could never tame it, and you sure couldn't control it.

1. What are some of the sources of pornography in our society? (Hint: Think about what you see and hear.)

   _____

   _____

   _____

2. What do you think pornography does to a person's mind?

   _____

   _____

   _____

   _____

   _____

Our minds act like computers and also like cameras. Just as a computer's response is based on the data programmed into it, whatever data we put into our minds will affect how we view the world and how we respond to it. It's not quite this simple because our minds are far more complex than any computer in the world, but the basic principles work the same way.

You have probably heard the phrase, "garbage in, garbage out." When we allow ourselves to view sexually explicit material, it's like downloading a computer virus into the hard-drive of our minds. Those images start to corrupt our thinking and how we react to other people.

Our minds are also like a camera because, when we look at a pornographic picture or movie, our minds record it—and store it to be brought back again and again.

3a. What does Romans 12:2 mean by "do not be conformed to this world"?

_____

_____

3b. What do you think "renewing of your mind" means?

_____

_____

_____

As we choose to draw near to God and yield our lives to the power of His Holy Spirit, He will give us the power NOT to conform to this world. As we allow God to reshape our defective thinking to align with His mind, our attitudes and actions will change. Life-change occurs from the inside out.

4.  What do you think this phrase means: "let us throw off everything that hinders and the sin that so easily entangles" (Hebrews 12:1b NIV)?

_____

_____

_____

Embracing temptation and viewing pornography is sin. Like other sins, it will weigh us down in every aspect of our lives. Did you know that pornography could easily become addicting, just like drinking alcohol or snorting cocaine? Addictions can kill you spiritually, mentally, and physically. The best way to avoid becoming addicted to something dangerous like pornography is to stay away from it altogether.

But that's not easy is it? Pornography is easily available today. Suddenly an ad comes on TV with a sexy woman wearing little of anything. Some of your friends bring a picture or magazine to school and ask you to look at it. You visit someone's house, only to find out that they plan to watch an 'R' rated movie that includes sexual scenes. Maybe a friend wants to show you a sex site on the Web.

5a. What would you do if something like this happened to you?

_____

_____

5b. Have any kids at school brought dirty pictures to school? Do any of them talk about seeing naked women on the Internet? What do you do when they say that?"

_____

_____

_____

> *Do not offer the parts of your body to sin, as instruments of wickedness, but rather offer yourselves to God, as those who have been brought from death to life; and offer the parts of your body to Him as instruments of righteousness.*
>
> Romans 6:13 (NIV)

6. According to Psalm 101:3, what should your stand be on pornography or any explicit images that tempt you?

_____

_____

7. What does God promise to offer you if you are willing to trust Him when you face a temptation (read 1 Corinthians 10:13)?

_____

_____

_____

*Hoplon* is a Greek term that refers to armor or weapons of warfare. Just as Teknon and Kratos need their armor to protect them in the battle, Christians also need armor—spiritual armor. The Bible describes this armor of God in Ephesians 6:10-18.

8. What makes up the spiritual armor that God provides for us ? How could this armor help you to gain more self-discipline in what you watch, listen to, and read?

_____

_____

_____

_____

_____

_____

These physical objects are metaphors representing God's gifts of protection and spiritual weapons that will help us in the battle against temptation. We need to put on God's full armor or we will not be ready to do battle with Satan. We must trust God and make the right choices in what we see, think, and do.

When you put on the armor of God, it's almost like Kratos putting on the Hoplon. God gives you all of the weapons you need to fight your enemy, Satan. Satan would like nothing more than for you to start a habit of looking at the pornographic or sensual material so that your relationship with God and other people would be hindered.

9.  What do you think are some of the benefits of not looking at pornography?

_____

_____

_____

Let's get practical. Here are some suggestions that will help you gain control over this area of your mind, now and in the future. But, to gain control of your mind, you have to make the right choices, even when you're alone.

*Movies.* Set a standard for what movie rating levels you will not watch. Using the movie rating standards is tough because some "R" rated films are not as bad as some of those rated "PG-13" or even "PG". But, remember, a film that carries a "PG-13" or "R" rating does so for a reason. You can save yourself a lot of headaches and uncomfortable situations with your friends, by telling them you have decided to stay away from these ratings. You can and should check with your father about which movies are acceptable to watch. The real standard you need, God's standard, is found in Philippians 4:8.

Dwell or think only on things that meet God's standard—the PHIL 4:8 standard:

Whatever is:

- true
- honorable
- right
- pure
- lovely
- admirable
- excellent
- worthy of praise

*Videos.* The same suggestions apply here. This category is far more available and will require integrity on your part, especially when you are at a friend's house and his parents are gone.

*Magazines.* Obviously, you need to avoid pornographic magazines like the plague. But, you also need to be careful of publications that are not openly focused on sex, yet talk a lot about it. Reading these magazines and looking at the pictures can entice you to look at something worse. Remember the Shocktech problem—"Error increases with distance."

*Cable Television.* With more channels comes more opportunity to watch the wrong stuff. Plan ahead of time, which shows you will watch, and which ones you won't. Channel surfing is a dangerous sport; don't play it!

*Internet.* Every computer needs neon signs around it that flash, "Beware, hazardous roads ahead!" Before you start 'surfing' on the 'Super Highway', do yourself a favor and have your parents set the controls to prevent entry to the bad sites. Be purposeful. Decide which information you need, get it, and get out. The Internet has already ruined many men's minds because of careless surfing. And be careful of chat rooms. Even chat rooms geared toward young people can take off in a sexual direction without advance notice.

*Music.* What you hear can influence you as much as what you watch. Stay away from music that describes sexual intimacy and violence. And don't let yourself get drawn into the trap of watching music videos on cable channels.

*Video Games.* Whether at home or at the arcade, video games are becoming more violent and more sexually suggestive. Don't let yourself get sucked into the never-ending spiral of destructive competition that these games offer.

Setting high standards for what you watch, read, and listen to is a lot like racing toward that cliff Kratos described a few episodes ago. The best time to put on the brakes is when you know the cliff *is* ahead. The danger from pornography, like the cliff, is ahead. Remember your part in the CHAMPION Ring and take the responsibility to set high standards. Decide to put on your brakes now by refusing to look at any of pornography. Also trust God to give you the strength to turn away from this material and to encircle you with his ring of protection even before the pictures or words cross your path. Ask your father or mother, and one of your trusted Christian friends, to pray for you and make sure you are holding the line in this area.

Take heart if you have already failed or even developed a bad habit in this area. Remember that God loves you and is waiting for you to seek His forgiveness. Don't let the guilt that so often comes with this habit overtake you and make you depressed. You can restore fellowship with God today and draw on His strength to help you kick the habit. Jesus said, "I have overcome the world" (John 16:33). Since He has overcome the world, He can help you overcome your habits and tendencies. Be courageous enough to share your difficulties with your father today and ask him to help you.

Don't pet the T-Rex of pornography. At first, it may purr like a kitten, but sooner or later it will bite like a Savannah Monitor.

> *I do not pray for success. I ask for faithfulness.*
>
> Mother Teresa

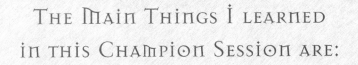

## The Main Things I learned in this Champion Session are:

_____

_____

_____

_____

_____

## CHAMPION
### Sheet of Deeds

Go to the CHAMPION Sheet of Deeds on page 9 and write down **one thing you will begin to do** before the next session (and beyond) to apply the main things you learned in session 7.

# Your Mission

Complete your mission and CHAMPION Session Prep before you meet for session 8.

## Power Verse: Psalm 101:3

**Date memorized:** _____

## Critical Maneuver

This will reinforce what you learned in this session. Obtain your maneuver instructions from your father.

## CHAMPION Sheet of Deeds

Begin to apply your action point from your Sheet of Deeds.

## CHAMPION Session Prep

Reread episode 8 of *Teknon and the CHAMPION Warriors*, and then complete the questions in session 8 in your *Mission Guide* on your own. **Our next CHAMPION Session will be:**

**DATE:**

_____

**TIME:**

_____

**PLACE:**

_____

# Special Topic Note Pages

# SPECIAL TOPIC NOTE PAGES

# Session 8:
# Faced With Fear

## CHAMPION Characteristic

**Courage**

POWER VERSE:  Joshua 1:9 (NIV)

*Have I not commanded you?  Be strong and courageous.  Do not be terrified; do not be discouraged, for the Lord your God will be with you wherever you go.*

# Discussion Topics

**Overcoming fear of rejection and fear of failure**
**Learning to recover from failure—part 2**

1. Discuss your mission from session 7. What did you learn from your maneuver? How is what you've learned affecting your attitude or behavior?

   _____

2. How will you continue to apply all of your action points from the Sheet of Deeds thus far? The goal for these is to see some habit patterns changing in your life. Are any changes occurring as you continue to apply all your various actions points?

   _____

   _____

3. Recite your power verse (Psalm 101:3) from session 7.

4a. Have you been more aware of areas where you need to be more careful in what you set before your eyes or hear with your ears? What are you doing to protect yourself in the following areas? (Exercise your responsibility within the CHAMPION's Ring.)

   ■ Movies

   ■ The Internet

   ■ Video games

   ■ Television

   ■ Music

   ■ Magazines

4b. When you are faced with an opportunity to look at pornography, what will you do to gain God's strength to resist that temptation? (What's in God's Ring?)

_____

_____


5. Recite the CHAMPION Warrior Creed. Say it as you would to a group of people; speak slowly and clearly.

# RECONNAISSANCE

1. Review the Map of the Mission on page 8 and determine the team's location in episode 8.

2. Review the CHAMPION definition of **Courage**. (Refer to the CHAMPION Code on page 6.)

_____

_____


3. What happened to Teknon during the team's fight with the footsoldiers?

_____

_____


4. Why do you think Teknon responded the way he did during the battle?

_____

_____

5. How did Teknon feel about his performance during the battle? Why?

_____

_____

6. How did the footsoldier manage to hurt Kratos?

_____

---

### OPTIONAL QUESTIONS

7. Could Kratos have prevented getting injured by the footsoldier? If so, how?

_____

8. The CHAMPION Warriors worked well as a team. When you face problems, why is teamwork so important?

_____

_____

---

9. What did Epps mean when he said, "It takes time to learn how to respond correctly in battle."?

_____

_____

10. Epps also coached Teknon that, "You learn by doing." How does this apply to Teknon?

_____

_____

# STRATEGY AND TACTICS

*The size of a person is determined by what it takes to stop him.*

Dr. Howard Hendricks

Failure is an essential part of life. It can also be an expensive part of life. At the end of the movie "Apollo 13," actor Tom Hanks quotes his character, astronaut Jim Lovell with this statement: "They called Apollo 13 a successful failure. We didn't make it to the moon, but we returned safely."

Gene Krantz, mission control specialist of Apollo 13, vented his frustration at two other NASA officials after hearing them discuss the potential, impending disaster to the space program after this setback. "Excuse me gentlemen," he barked. "I believe this will be our finest hour."

Failure has two faces. There are *successful* failures, and there are *unsuccessful* failures. Apollo 13 was a successful failure. Not only did the astronauts return home safely under incredibly difficult circumstances, they also exercised a high level of creative output and genuine teamwork over a period of only five days that rivals any single human endeavor of the century.

## LEARNING TO RECOVER

Dave Simmons, former linebacker of the Dallas Cowboys, had an interesting football philosophy that applies to the rest of life too. He said, "Every play is a game; learn to recover, recover, recover."

Simmons explained in his seminar *Dad the Family Shepherd* that every play during a football game is like a game in itself. The team plans for the play, gets information for the play, and then executes the play. Usually the play is a success. Sometimes it's not. Whether or not the play is successful, the team must come back and execute again.

Let's say it's second down and ten yards to go. The quarterback throws a short pass over the middle. His eyes widen because it's almost intercepted. If it had been intercepted, the cornerback on the other team would have run for a touchdown. After the play, the quarterback is back in the huddle. What is he going to think? What is he going to do?

*In great attempts, it is glorious even to fail.*

Vince Lombardi

The quarterback has to do three things. (1) He must learn from his mistake of throwing the ball late. (2) He must decide what he is going to do on the next play. (3) He must recover from the mistake and move on to the next play! The more he plays, the less he will make that mistake again. What would happen if he said to himself, *Gosh, I shouldn't have thrown that pass; it was almost intercepted. I guess I just shouldn't play football.* Nonsense!

There are times when failure is a natural consequence of living. In fact, God often uses trials and failures as a learning process in our lives. When He does this, we learn, as Epps said, by doing. In James 1:2-4 the NIV Bible tells us, "Consider it pure joy, my brothers, when you face trials of many kinds, because you know that the testing of your faith develops perseverance. Perseverance must finish its work so that you may be mature and complete, not lacking anything."

There are times, however, when we fail because we run from responsibility. Sometimes we run because we aren't prepared for the challenge we face. Sometimes we run because we fear the criticism we might receive from our peers as a result of taking the responsibility. And sometimes we run because we fear the possibility of failure.

## Failure, Forgiveness, and Fortification

Failure can have another name—sin. Sin, simply put, is falling short of God's perfect standard, which results in broken fellowship with Him. Whether we sin by active disobedience or rebellion, or by passive indifference, the result is the same. But we can recover from this type of failure and make it successful.

When we avoid responsibility, we must get back into the game as soon as possible. The recovery progresses in three stages:

I. **Failure:** We make the wrong decision, do the wrong thing, or find ourselves unable to succeed in a task.

II. **Forgiveness:** If sin is involved, we seek to restore fellowship with God by asking His forgiveness for our mistake. Then we forgive ourselves for our poor choice and weakness. We also seek forgiveness from people we have hurt.

III. **Fortification:** We recognize God's forgiveness for our failure and His grace for our limitations, learn from our mistakes, and try again.

*If we confess our sins, He [God] is faithful and righteous to forgive us our sins and to cleanse us from all unrighteousness.*

1 John 1:9

◆ Teknon and the Champion Warriors ◆

The Bible describes how the apostle Peter recovered after failing Jesus several times.

1. Check out Matthew 16:21-23. How did Peter respond toward Jesus and his prediction of his own suffering and death? How did Jesus respond to Peter?

_____

_____

_____

2a. According to Luke 22:54-62, what did Peter do when Jesus was on the verge of being crucified?

_____

_____

2b. What do you think Peter's responsibility was to Jesus in this situation?

_____

_____

2c. Why do you think Peter ran from responsibility and failed Jesus in His time of need?

_____

_____

_____

3. Read John 21:15-19 and Acts 2:38-47. Was Peter able to recover from his failures to obey and follow Christ? How do you know?

_____

_____

_____

Peter was one of Jesus' closest friends. In fact, Jesus referred to Peter as the "Rock" because of his faith and strength of character. When Jesus told Peter that all of His friends would eventually deny him, Peter promised that he would never do such a thing. And yet, Peter ran from his responsibility on the night Jesus was crucified. When asked about his friendship with Christ, Peter denied that he even knew Jesus three times!

"What a cowardly failure Peter was!" we might say. How could he recover from such a mistake? Well, he not only sought forgiveness from God for his mistake, but he went on to become one of the most powerful preachers the world has ever known. Peter recovered!

4. Have you ever felt like a failure the way Teknon felt after the battle? Do you think God understands that you aren't perfect?

_____

_____

5. Read Psalm 103:13-14 and 1 Corinthians 1:25-27. What do these verses teach us about our own strength and God's understanding of how we're put together?

_____

_____

_____

*Even though large tracts of Europe have fallen or may fall into the grip of the Gestapo and all the odious apparatus of Nazi rule, we shall not flag nor fail. We shall go on to the end, we shall fight in France, we shall fight on the seas and the oceans, we shall fight with growing confidence and growing strength in the air, we shall defend our island, whatever the cost may be ... we shall never surrender.*

Winston Churchill (before Parliament in June 1940)

God knows that we make mistakes. He knows us better than we know ourselves because He created us. If you've made a mistake you can recover. If you've run from responsibility, you can recover. If you've been criticized, you can recover. God has unlimited power to enable you to recover, recover, and recover again. Remember, successful failure is not a bad thing. But if your failure is a sin, you must admit your failure to God, choose not to make the bad choice again, and return to walking with God. If you do these things, He promises to restore you.

6. When, in your life, have you experienced a successful failure? How did you learn from, and recover from, that failure?

_____

_____

7. Describe one or two or your unsuccessful failures? How did you learn from, and recover from the failure?

_____

_____

8. As a result of what you've learned in this session, how will you handle successful and unsuccessful failures differently in the future?

_____

_____

Do you think that Teknon will learn how to recover and get back into the battle? Press on to episode 9 of the story.

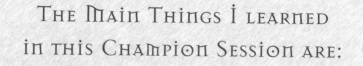

## The Main Things I learned in this Champion Session are:

_____

_____

_____

_____

_____

## CHAMPION
### Sheet of Deeds

Go to the CHAMPION Sheet of Deeds on page 9 and write down **one thing you will begin to do** before the next session (and beyond) to apply the main things you learned in session 8.

# Your Mission

Complete your mission and CHAMPION Session Prep before you meet for session 9.

## POWER VERSE: JOSHUA 1:9

Date memorized: _____

## CRITICAL MANEUVER

This will reinforce what you learned today. Obtain your maneuver instructions from your father.

## CHAMPION SHEET OF DEEDS

Begin to apply your action point from your Sheet of Deeds.

## CHAMPION SESSION PREP

Reread episode 9 of *Teknon and the CHAMPION Warriors*, and then complete session 9 in your *Mission Guide* on your own. **Our next CHAMPION Session:**

DATE:

_____

TIME:

_____

PLACE:

_____

# SESSION 9: RECOVER, RECOVER, RECOVER

## CHAMPION Characteristics
### Courage and Mental Toughness

POWER VERSE: PSALM 56:3-4

*When I am afraid, I will put my trust in You. In God, whose word I praise, in God I have put my trust; I shall not be afraid. What can mere man do to me?*

# Discussion Topics

**Breaking out of your "comfort zone"**

**Being respected vs. being liked**

**Recovering from failure—part 2: not giving in to discouragement**

1. Discuss your mission from session 8. Did you complete your maneuver? If so, what did you learn? If not, why not?

2. What are some habits you are successfully forming as you apply your action points from your Sheet of Deeds? Any areas of struggle?

3. Recite your power verse (Joshua 1:9) from session 8.

4. What is your greatest fear from among those you identified during your mission from session 8? What are some things you could do to overcome it (remember, the CHAMPION's Ring includes areas where you can make a difference)? What things do you need to trust to the Lord (responsibilities that rest in God's Ring)?

5. Recite the CHAMPION Warrior Creed out loud. Pause before you say the lines about courage and mental toughness.

# RECONNAISSANCE

1. Review the Map of the Mission on page 8 to determine the team's location in episode 9.

2. Review the CHAMPION definitions of **Courage** and **Mental Toughness** (refer to the CHAMPION Code on page 6).

_____

_____

_____

_____

---

## OPTIONAL QUESTIONS

3. What were Matty's three main instructions to Teknon?

_____

_____

4. How did Teknon motivate the Phaskos to join him?

_____

_____

---

5. Why did Teknon hesitate to go to the village? What was he afraid of?

_____

_____

6. Why did Tor tell Teknon not to worry about being liked by the Phaskos? What did Tor say about respect? What did he mean?

_____

_____

7. Look back at episode 4 where Teknon meets the Harpax. Do you think Teknon liked being liked? Why do you think acceptance by the Harpax was so important to Teknon?

_____

_____

_____

8. What did Scandalon do to Teknon on his way to the village? Why?

_____

_____

9. What did Teknon recognize about the strange voice he heard while he was leading the Phaskos back to the team?

_____

_____

10. Why did Teknon respond differently to Scandalon's voice on the way back to the clearing?

_____

_____

11. Why did Teknon want to keep the scar on his arm?

_____

_____

12. Do you think Teknon recovered from his failure in episode 8? If so, how?

_____

_____

# STRATEGY AND TACTICS

*Be on the alert, stand firm in the faith, act like men, be strong.*

1 Corinthians 16:13

## BREAK OUT OF THE ZONE!

Have you ever heard an athlete say, "I was in the zone"? For an athlete, being "in the zone" refers to playing a sport far beyond what he considers his normal ability. If you've had that experience, you know how good it feels to experience that kind of achievement. There's another zone, however, that also feels good, but for another reason. It's called the "comfort zone."

In the comfort zone, you feel good because you feel comfortable. The comfort zone is a place where you do things because it's the way you've always done them.

Let's say you are becoming a skilled trumpet player. One

morning the bandleader says to you, "How about playing a solo during our next concert?"

"No way," you blurt out. "I like playing with the other trumpet players just fine, thank you very much." There you are in the center of your comfort zone. You have an opportunity to grow, but you don't want to risk breaking out.

1. Have you ever been afraid to take on a particularly difficult task, to work closely with someone who really seems not to like you, or to ask for the help of someone who you are afraid to approach? Jot down a couple of examples.

_____

_____

We break out of our comfort zone by conquering our fears. When we conquer fears with God's help, we experience personal, emotional, and spiritual victory.

We will examine some important factors to remember when you want to break out of your comfort zone.

*Every noble work is at first impossible.*

Thomas Carlyle

## God Provides the Power to Break Out of the Zone

2a. What does King David tell you about who God is and what He does for you in Psalm 27:1,13-14?

_____

_____

_____

2b. What does Psalm 27:1,13-14 tell you not to do? What does it tell you that you should do?

_____

_____

# BREAKING OUT OF THE ZONE IS PROFITABLE BUT NOT ALWAYS POPULAR

Often, the biggest barrier to leaving the comfort zone is our own fear of what others might say. Nobody likes to be criticized, and nobody likes to be misunderstood. When we do something outside our comfort zone, like giving a speech or sharing our faith in God with someone else, we put our egos at risk. Let's face it: we like to be liked. But it is not always necessary to be liked by everyone. At times, people are going to misunderstand us. At other times, people will also become angry with us even when we do the right thing!

3. Read Psalm 56:3-4. If you trust in God, what can others do to you?

_____

_____

_____

_____

_____

4. What does Jesus warn us about living in this world in John 15:15-16? How should we expect to be liked and accepted if we are His friends and follow Him?

_____

_____

_____

_____

On May 20-21, 1927, Charles Lindbergh accomplished something many people thought was impossible. In fact, many people didn't understand why the young pilot would even attempt to fly solo across the Atlantic Ocean from New York to Paris. Today hundreds of planes fly transatlantic every day, but prior to 1927 several other pilots had met their deaths in similar transatlantic attempts. People tried to convince Lindbergh that death was waiting for him somewhere in the icy waters of the Atlantic. Many became angry and called him crazy. Fortunately, Lindbergh ignored his critics and showed the world that he and his famous plane, "The Spirit of St. Louis," had the right stuff. Today we recognize him as an American hero because of his unwillingness to allow circumstances or criticism to discourage him from reaching his dream.

In the same way, Scandalon hit Teknon with discouraging comments on his way to the village when he was trying to recover from failure. Our enemy (Satan) can use this tactic very effectively to keep us from recovering,

5.  Do you ever hear voices like this from other people or in your own thoughts? Underline the following comments that sound familiar.

    ■ Don't tell me you're going to speak in front of the class today. Are you nuts?!
    ■ Forget trying out for the team. You don't stand a chance.
    ■ Why do you want to make good grades? No one else does.
    ■ You mean you haven't kissed a girl yet? What are you, some kind of freak?
    ■ Share your faith? What if the person laughs at you?
    Any others? Write them here:

    _____

As Teknon returned to the clearing, he recognized that Scandalon's voice was a trick. He determined that the voices he heard were a lie and did not apply to him. Then he changed his mental course by ignoring those false messages.

6. What does 2 Timothy 1:7 say about fear?

_____

_____

_____

_____

7. What does Jesus say about the truth (God's Word) in John 8:32?

_____

_____

_____

When you hear false voices, replace them with the truth of God's Word. If you have invited Christ into your life by faith, you are child of the King. Neither people nor Satan's messengers can intimidate you unless you let them.

According to Henry Blackaby and Claude King, authors of *Experiencing God*, God is working all around us. When we seek to develop our personal relationship with Him, which began when we invited Him into our lives by faith, He provides opportunities to join Him where He is working. These invitations usually take us out of our comfort zone. But if we step outside the zone (remember the CHAMPION's Ring on the Hoplon) and allow God to accomplish what only He can (God's Ring), we grow as individuals as well as in our relationship with Him.

## BREAKING OUT OF THE ZONE IS WORTH THE RISK

At times, God asks us to step out of our comfort zone to obey His will. We may not know how we are going to accomplish it, but we know that He wants it done. That's when God expects us to trust in Him by faith and watch Him bring about the results.

8. Read Matthew 17:20. If we have faith in God, what does He say that we can do? How much faith do we need in order to see God do mighty things?

_____

_____

_____

We can have faith in God is because He is faithful. He is all-powerful and loves you unconditionally. If God provides you an opportunity to leave your comfort zone, He will give you the power to break out of it. Philippians 4:13 reminds us that "I can do all things through Him [Jesus Christ] who gives me strength."

We grow by taking the risk to trust God in our daily lives. God loves us and wants us to grow—in our relationship with Him, in our understanding of ourselves, and in our relationships with other people. Just like Teknon received help to accomplish his rescue mission, we can trust God to provide the power to accomplish whatever mission He gives us when we ask for His help. We may not always see His answer right away. Sometimes God wants us to wait patiently; He wants us to learn through waiting, even though it's difficult. But we can always be confident that He knows our concerns and wants the best for us.

Remember when Tor told Teknon to look at his scar often, and never to forget what he had learned that night? Faith often involves risk—risk to our self-esteem and maybe even to our friendships. Sometimes we have to risk getting hurt by other people. But when we conquer our fears, step out of our comfort zone, and trust God through the experience, we will receive a feeling of exhilaration and a memory of victory that will stay with us forever!

9. Name three activities that would take you out of your comfort zone.

(1) _____

(2) _____

(3) _____

## The Main Things I learned in this Champion Session are:

_____

_____

_____

_____

_____

> *You gain strength, courage, and confidence by every experience in which you really stop to look fear in the face ... You must do the thing you think you cannot do.*
>
> Eleanor Roosevelt

## CHAMPION
### Sheet of Deeds

Go to the **CHAMPION** Sheet of Deeds on page 9 and write down **one thing you will begin to do** before the next session (and beyond) to apply the main things you learned in session 9.

# Your Mission

Complete your mission and CHAMPION Session Prep before you meet for session 10.

## Power Verse: Psalm 56:3-4

**Date memorized:** _____

## Critical Maneuver

This will reinforce what you learned today.  Obtain your maneuver instructions from your father.

## CHAMPION Sheet of Deeds

Begin to apply your action point from your Sheet of Deeds.

## CHAMPION Session Prep

Reread episode 10 of *Teknon and the CHAMPION Warriors*, and then complete the questions in session 10 in your *Mission Guide* on your own.  Our next CHAMPION Session will be:

DATE:

_____

TIME:

_____

PLACE:

_____

# Session 10:
# Good Enough

## CHAMPION Characteristics
**Attitude and Integrity**

### POWER VERSE: 1 CORINTHIANS 9:24–25A

*Do you not know that those who run in a race all run, but only one receives the prize? Run in such a way that you may win. Everyone who competes in the games exercises self-control in all things.*

# Discussion Topics

**Pursuing excellence and resisting mediocrity**
**Managing your anger**

1. Discuss your mission from session 9. What was the most important thing you learned from your maneuver?

   _____

   _____

2. Name one key thing that you have learned so far by applying your action points from the Sheet of Deeds.

   _____

   _____

3. Recite your power verse (Psalm 56:3-4) from session 9.

4. This power verse reveals that we should not fear people. Is there any person or group of people you fear? Why? What can you do to face this fear?

   _____

   _____

   _____

   _____

5. Recite the CHAMPION Warrior Creed together from memory (see page 5).

# Reconnaissance

1. Review the Map of the Mission on page 8 to determine the team's location in episode 10.

2. Review CHAMPION definition of **Integrity**.

_____

_____

_____

_____

3. What does the phrase "I will allow other people to hold me accountable to standards of excellence" mean to you?

_____

_____

_____

4. Phil said that the Northrons enjoyed mediocrity. How is this revealed in their lives?

_____

_____

_____

5. Tor said that the Northrons "have no vision ... no purpose ... no plan." He said, "Where there's no purpose, there's no passion for living." Why is it important to have vision, purpose, and a plan in our lives?

_____

_____

_____

---

## ⊙ptiⓞnal Questiⓞns

6. *Northros*, a Greek term, refers to being slothful, sluggish, or lazy. Why was this community called Northros?

_____

---

7. Why did Tor lose his temper?

_____

_____

8. Do you think that Tor had a right to get angry? Why or why not? Was it right for him to hurt the Northron? Why do you see it that way?

_____

_____

9. How did Tor feel after he lost his temper? What did he do after he hurt the Northron? Why?

_____

_____

10. What did Epps say was a sign of true strength in Tor? What did Epps mean by that?

_____

_____

11. *Tharreo* is a Greek word that refers to having courage, confidence, and boldness. Tor is a task-driven leader; one who likes to be in authority. How does he show his courage?

_____

_____

_____

# STRATEGY AND TACTICS

## RAISE THE BAR, ROCK THE BOAT, BUT DON'T ROLL WITH THE TIDE

You decide to make better grades this semester. To make this happen, you will need to work harder and pay more attention in class. When your friends find out what you're doing, what might they say?

"JUST CHILL OUT!"

You choose to get into excellent physical shape. You will have to run and work out with weights three times a week. Some of your friends who don't exercise hear about this. What might they say?

"JUST CHILL OUT!"

You sense that God wants you to share your faith with some non-Christians. But in order to do that, you'll need to learn how to share your testimony of how you became a Christian, as well as how to lead another person into a relationship with Jesus.

What might you hear even from some of your Christian friends?

"JUST CHILL OUT!"

Many teens and adults don't appreciate someone who wants to pursue excellence in his life. They don't like it when a person rocks the boat by using self-discipline and extra effort to set—and reach—worthwhile goals. A Northron-type mentality seems to be sweeping through our homes and schools.

Apparently, "good enough" is enough for many people.

How about you? Do you like being mediocre? Do you accept low standards for yourself? Do you hesitate to raise the bar of your goals and expectations because it will set you apart from others? Or is it just too much effort to be better than "good enough"?

1. Revelation 3:15-16 describes the church at Laodicea. What kind of attitude is Jesus describing here? And what is His response toward this type of attitude?

_____

_____

_____

2a. According to Ephesians 5:15-17, how should we use our time?

_____

_____

_____

2b. What do you think it means to "make the most of every opportunity"?

_____

_____

_____

3. Read Luke 2:40-52. In what ways was Jesus growing as a person even though He was only 12 years old?

_____

_____

_____

God expects us to be thankful for the talents and opportunities He gives us. He also expects us to make the most of the life and gifts He has provided. The story in Luke 2 declares that Jesus grew and kept increasing in stature (physically), in wisdom (mentally), in favor with men (socially), and in favor with God (spiritually). Jesus was a good steward of what God the Father had entrusted to Him. He set an example for us to keep increasing in our maturity by avoiding mediocrity in our lives.

4. In Matthew 19:26 what does Jesus say is possible with God?

_____

_____

5. Read Philippians 4:13.  If we are Christians, what can we do as a result of God's power working through us?

_____

_____

If nothing is impossible with God, and you can do all things through Him as He gives you His strength, how should you approach your activities?  Ask yourself these questions:

- Am I trying to learn everything that I can at school?
- Do I do my chores at home completely, without grumbling?
- Am I exercising and being careful what I eat?
- Am I reading good books on a regular basis?
- Am I learning how to interact well with people and treating them kindly?
- Am I consistent in spending time with God in prayer and Bible reading?
- Do I know how to share my faith?
- Do I look for opportunities to share my faith?

These questions refer to attitudes and behaviors that are your responsibility within the CHAMPION's Ring (see session 1).  You can and should take responsibility to make the right choices in areas such as study, work, exercise, learning, and so on.

Don't allow yourself to fall into the Northron "good enough" mentality and don't be afraid to rock the boat of mediocrity.  God will do His part (God's Ring), so trust Him to help you raise the bar in the different areas of your life.  You don't have to roll with the tide of what everybody else is doing.  "Aim high," as the Air Force says.  Pursue excellence and let someone else do the chilling out!

## USE YOUR HEAD; DON'T LOSE YOUR HEAD!

Do you have a short fuse?  When people disagree with you or fail to meet your expectations does your response resemble the fireworks display at Walt Disney World?  How often do you lose your patience or "blow up" with other people?

It's almost fashionable to have a short fuse, isn't it? More and more people seem to be adopting the attitude of "I'm mad and I'm not going to take it anymore!" as their creed for social interaction. Even violent anger is recognized as the status quo.

## OPTIONAL QUESTIONS

6a. What makes you angry? How do you handle it when it erupts?

_____

6b. Does any particular person make you angry? Why? How do you handle it when this person makes you angry?

_____

_____

7. Review the CHAMPION definition of Attitude (refer to "The CHAMPION Code" on page 6).

_____

_____

8. How do you think a person learns to manage anger?

_____

_____

The Bible talks about the process of managing anger as a key component of self-control. Self-control is one of the outward expressions of Christ's presence in our lives as we learn to trust our lives to Him. The Bible calls these characteristics the "fruit of the Spirit."

9. Read Galatians 5:22-23. What is the fruit of the Spirit?

_____

_____

_____

_____

Uncontrolled anger, like so many other things, can become a habit. Once you get used to "losing your head" it becomes easier to let it happen the next time. Tor had a habit of losing his temper until he decided to become a CHAMPION Warrior. He knew that self-control was a key characteristic of a CHAMPION and didn't want to accept "good enough" in his life.

If you are a Christian, God expects you to overcome a bad temper by drawing on His power. We plug into His strength by being filled with His Spirit. When you are filled with the Holy Spirit, you start displaying the fruit of the Spirit. It is one thing to hate evil and become angered by its presence in the world. It's another thing to take out frustrations on others. When we do that, we disobey God. If you sense that you have disobeyed God through a fit of bad temper, remember 1 John 1:9 and confess your anger to Him. He will forgive you and reestablish His line of communication and power with you.

But we could spend our lives trying to manage anger after it has erupted. How do we keep from losing our temper ahead of time? The book of James describes an effective formula for anger prevention.

10. Read James 1:19-20. What three things should we do to keep from losing our temper?

Write the formula here:

God's Power + _____ + _____

+ _____ = Anger Management

Emmett John Hughes, a friend of former President Eisenhower gave him this advice: "Never miss an opportunity to keep your mouth shut."

Keeping our mouths shut is one of the hardest things in the world to do when we get upset. It's also one of the most effective tools in anger management. A spoken word is like a football right before it's intercepted. As much as the quarterback wants it back, he can't get it back. If there is any question whether or not you should say something, listen to what Mr. Hughes said to the president. DON'T SAY IT!

Instead of being quick to speak, use the other highly effective tool in anger management. Learn to listen. Author Stephen Covey says, "Seek first to understand, then to be understood." Listen not only to what's being said, but also to what isn't being said. Try to put yourself in the other person's shoes so you can better understand his or her position.

God knows that you get angry; He created anger to alert you that something is wrong. But when you get angry, draw on His strength to remain calm and under the control of His Spirit. Use your head; don't lose your head!

# The Main Things I learned in this Champion Session are:

_____

_____

_____

_____

_____

> *Don't fly into a rage unless you are prepared for a rough landing.*
>
> Anonymous

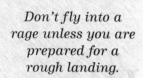

## CHAMPION SHEET OF DEEDS

Go to the CHAMPION Sheet of Deeds on page 9 and write down **one thing you will begin to do** before the next session (and beyond) to apply the main things you learned in session 10.

# Your Mission

Complete your mission and CHAMPION Session Prep before you meet for session 11.

## POWER VERSE: I CORINTHIANS 9:24-25A

Date memorized: _____

## CRITICAL MANEUVER

Your father will give you instructions for your maneuver.

## CHAMPION SHEET OF DEEDS

Begin to apply your action point from your Sheet of Deeds.

## CHAMPION SESSION PREP

Reread episode 11 of *Teknon and the CHAMPION Warriors*, and then complete the questions in session 11 of your *Mission Guide* on your own. **Our next CHAMPION Session will be:**

DATE:

TIME:

PLACE:

# Session 11:
# The Element of Doubt

## Champion Characteristics
**Integrity and Purity**

Power Verse: 1 Thessalonians 5:21-22

*But examine everything carefully; hold fast to that which is good; abstain from every form of evil.*

# Discussion Topics

**Knowing who I am and what my personal convictions are**
**Living out my convictions**
**Avoiding romantic relationships and entanglements**

## Mission Debrief

1. Discuss your mission from session 10. What was the most important thing you learned from your maneuver?

_____

_____

2. What changes are happening in your life as you apply your action points from the CHAMPION Sheet of Deeds? Share some victories you are seeing.

_____

_____

3. Recite your power verse (1 Corinthians 9:24-25a) from session 10.

4. Name at least one area in which you have executed self-control since your last CHAMPION session.

_____

_____

5. Recite the CHAMPION Warrior Creed from memory. If you can, invite two or more people to be in the room when you say it.

# RECONNAISSANCE

1. Review the Map of the Mission on page 8 before beginning this section. Identify where the team is located in episode 11.

2. Review the CHAMPION definitions of **Integrity** and **Purity** (refer to the CHAMPION Code on page 6).

_____

_____

_____

_____

3. How did Magos try to confuse Teknon?

_____

_____

_____

4. What did Magos offer Teknon?

_____

_____

_____

5. Why do you think Magos challenged Teknon about his beliefs?  What did Epps have to say about this?

_____

_____

_____

_____

_____

> *Magos wanted to create doubt in your mind about your beliefs, so that you would feel frightened and insecure.*
>
> Epps

6. Why did Teknon enjoy spending time with Pary?

_____

_____

7. In what way(s) did Teknon's encounter with Magos affect his decision to see Pary again?

_____

_____

8. Describe how Teknon treated Pary during the three days they spent together.

_____

_____

9. After his conversation with Epps, what did Teknon realize that he had done wrong?

_____

_____

_____

10. How did Pary respond when Teknon talked with her that last morning on the beach?  Why did she react this way?

_____

_____

_____

11. How could Teknon have prevented this from happening and still maintained his friendship with Pary?

_____

_____

# STRATEGY AND TACTICS

# Be Willing to Get a Bloody Nose

Several years ago, a guy in his twenties named Brad got a job with a medical company selling surgical equipment. He spent the first six weeks training with that company in Chicago, learning everything he could about how to sell his company's products to hospitals and surgeons. One day during training, the vice-president sat down with Brad in the cafeteria. Trying to make conversation, Brad asked, "What would you do if you were starting out as a salesman again?" The executive's response was simple:

> "I'd get out in the field and get my nose bloody. That's the way you learn this business."

What was he saying to Brad? Did the vice-president mean that his new salesman should go back and try to start fights with doctors? No, he didn't have enough insurance for that! The executive was telling the young salesman that he needed to talk with his customers, try to meet the customers' needs, face stiff competition from other salesmen, allow himself to get challenged about what he had learned in training, and be willing to fail a few times as he started his new career. The vice-president knew that challenge isn't a bad thing. Challenge is a good thing.

*An expert at anything was once a beginner.*

H. Jackson Browne

1. Have you ever felt overly confident about a particular subject or task?

_____

_____

Author and speaker Stephen Covey often says, "Confidence is what you have before you understand the problem." It's important for each of us to realize that when we start out doing something new and important, we'll probably be challenged. Even if we feel confident about what we are learning, we don't know how *little* we know until we get *challenged* about what we know. When we get challenged on a topic, like Magos challenged Teknon, we have a great opportunity to reaffirm what we believe about that topic and to identify the things we don't know about it. Once we learn what we don't know, we can go and find the answers we need.

Magos gave Teknon a "bloody nose" by confusing him about his beliefs and convictions. Teknon became flustered and upset because he allowed Magos to inject the element of doubt into his mind. And because Teknon didn't immediately have an answer for Magos, he lost his confidence. Could Teknon have prevented Magos from frightening him like that?

A temptation to compromise your standards often comes when your beliefs are challenged. Let's look at another person who was challenged and offered a proposition by someone evil like Magos.

2a. Read Luke 4:1-13. Who was challenged? —and by whom?

_____

_____

2b. Considering that Jesus ate nothing during His time in the desert (verses 1-2), how do you think He felt when He was being challenged?

_____

_____

> *Reject passivity, accept responsibility, lead courageously, and expect God's reward.*
>
> Robert Lewis

2c. How did Jesus respond to the temptations and challenges made to Him?

| Verses to consider | Temptation/Challenge | Jesus' response |
|---|---|---|
| Luke 4:3-4 | | |
| Luke 4:5-8 | | |
| Luke 4:9-12 | | |

Jesus was very tired and hungry when Satan challenged His beliefs. But instead of becoming unsettled when Satan tried to use the element of doubt, Jesus quoted Scripture to strengthen his position. He confidently relied on the words of His Heavenly Father.

If you have accepted Jesus as your personal Savior by faith, sooner or later you will get challenged about why you believe in Jesus. If that happens, great! You will have the opportunity to go back to the Bible to find the answers to the challenges given to you. By doing that, you will fuel your confidence and reinforce your position in Christ! If you need help, ask your parents, your pastor, or someone else whom you respect to point you to Bible verses and other Bible-based materials that apply to your situation.

Better yet, even when someone else is *not* challenging you, spend time reading and studying the Bible now so that you will become more knowledgeable about what it means to be a Christian and apply God's truth each day.

3.  Most everyone has asked himself or herself, "What will my friends think if I stand up for what I believe?" Why is that such an important question to us?

_____

_____

_____

Build your character based on what God's Word has to say about His character. Don't get rattled like Teknon. He got stressed out over Magos' challenge, decided to take a break from reality in order to make himself feel better, and hurt himself and Pary in the process ... which leads us to our second topic.

## AVOID THE GUSH!

Here's what God says about relationships:

"Learn to love appropriately. You need to use your head and test your feelings so that your love is sincere and intelligent, not sentimental gush." Philippians 1:9-10 (The Message)

4.  It's nice when a girl shows you affection, isn't it?  What could
    be more pleasant than when she calls you on the phone and
    tells you how great you are?  It makes you feel good, doesn't it?
    But when you feel that way, whose needs are you meeting—
    yours or hers?  Are you being sincere and intelligent, or are
    you giving in to sentimental gush?

    _____

    _____

    _____

Emotions can be weird and funny things.  When emotions get
involved in a relationship between a young man and a young
woman, friends start to become more than friends.  Often at that
point people start getting hurt.

5a. Read 1 Timothy 5:1-2.  How are you supposed to treat young
    women if you will honor her and honor God?

    _____

    _____

    _____

    _____

5b. Is it wise for me to be anything other than a friend to what
    the Bible calls my sisters in the Lord?  Why or why not?

    _____

    _____

    _____

    _____

In his excellent book, *I Kissed Dating Goodbye,* Joshua Harris has this to say about romantic relationships:

> "I've come to realize that I have no business asking for a girl's heart and affections if I'm not ready to back up my request with a lifelong commitment. Until I can do that, I'd only be using that woman to meet my short-term needs, not seeking to bless her for the long term."

*A lifelong commitment???  Wait a minute!* you may be thinking. *I'm not talking about a lifelong commitment!  I just want to talk on the phone for a while.  Or go to the movies.  Or out to eat.  Just have a little fun.*

Sounds crazy doesn't it?  But even now, if you're not careful, you can misuse a romantic relationship with a young woman in order to meet your short-term needs instead of blessing her for the long term.  Remember Teknon and Pary?  Teknon just wanted to get away from it all for a few days.  But instead, a "perceived" romantic relationship was created and Pary was hurt as a result.

The pressure to start dating and to begin relationships is occurring earlier in life than ever before.  Don't allow yourself to start something romantic that you can't and shouldn't finish.  Instead, seek to treat young women as cherished sisters, friends whom you can encourage.  Don't get caught up in the gush because there is so much more to enjoy at this point by being friends.  This delayed gratification (waiting for what I want until God gives it to me at the right time) will become tougher as the years go by, but God will bless you for making the right decisions.  And your effort will be greatly rewarded—beyond whatever you could ask or think!  God promises this in Ephesians 3:20.  Check it out.

6.  What do you think would cause a girl to like you?

_____

7.  Describe what you think a friendship with a girl should be like?

_____

_____

_____

# The Main Things I learned in this Champion Session are:

_____

_____

_____

_____

_____

## CHAMPION
### Sheet of Deeds

Go to The CHAMPION Sheet of Deeds on page 9 and write down **one thing you will begin to do** before the next session (and beyond) to apply the main things you learned in session 11.

# Your Mission

Complete your mission and CHAMPION Session Prep before you meet for session 12.

## Power verse: 1 Thessalonians 5:21-22

**Date memorized:** _____

## Critical Maneuver

This will reinforce what you learned in this session. Obtain your maneuver instructions from your father.

## CHAMPION Sheet of Deeds

Begin to apply your action point from your Sheet of Deeds.

## CHAMPION Session Prep

Reread Episode 12 of *Teknon and the CHAMPION Warriors*, and then complete the questions in Session 12 in your *Mission Guide* on your own. **Our next CHAMPION Session will be:**

DATE:

TIME:

PLACE:

COURAGE · HONOR · ATTITUDE · MENTAL TOUGHNESS · PURITY · INTEGRITY · OWNERSHIP · NAVIGATION

# SESSION 12:
# NOTHING MORE,
# NOTHING LESS,
# NOTHING ELSE

## CHAMPION Characteristic
### Attitude

POWER VERSE: 1 CORINTHIANS 15:57–58

*But thanks be to God, who gives us the victory through our Lord Jesus Christ. Therefore, my beloved brethren, be steadfast, immovable, always abounding in the work of the Lord, knowing that your toil is not in vain in the Lord.*

# DiSCUSSiON TOPiCS:

**Managing discouragement**

**Keeping circumstances and self-perception
in proper perspective**

**Drawing on God's strength and wisdom**

# Mission Debrief

1.  Discuss your mission from session 11. What did you learn from your maneuver? Has your attitude or behavior changed as a result of your maneuver?

   _____

   _____

2.  Are you experiencing any struggles as you apply your action points from the CHAMPION Sheet of Deeds? If so, please share these.

   _____

   _____

3.  Recite your power verse (1 Thessalonians 5:21-22) from session 11.

4.  Our last session explored the topic of romantic relationships. Do you have a romantic relationship with a young woman right now? If so, should the relationship continue as it is? Why or why not?

   _____

   _____

5. Recite all of the CHAMPION Warrior Creed from memory (see page 5).

# RECONNAISSANCE

1. Review the Map of the Mission on page 8 and determine the team's location in episode 12.

2. Review the CHAMPION definition of **Attitude** (refer to the CHAMPION Code on page 6).

_____

_____

_____

3. What were some of the reasons Teknon became frustrated and angry?

_____

_____

4. What were some of the things that contributed to Teknon's discouragement?

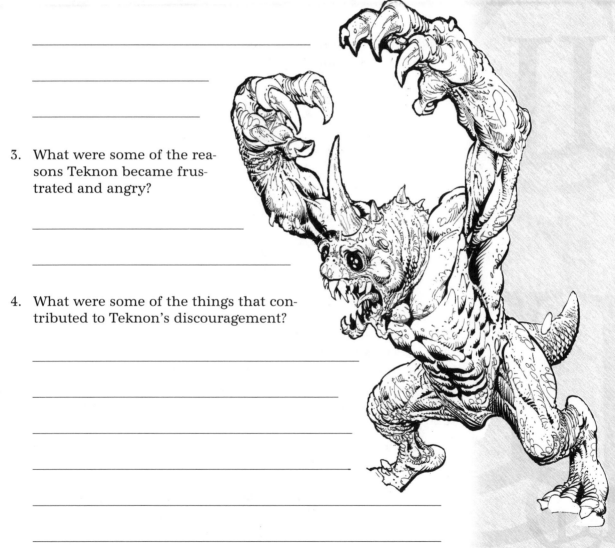

_____

_____

_____

_____

_____

5.  How did Teknon act when he became discouraged?
    Be specific.

    _____

6.  What, according to Kratos and Phil, is the way to overcome
    discouragement?

    _____

    _____

    _____

7.  Phil told Teknon, "Even when our emotions tell us otherwise,
    we must stay focused on trusting Pneuma to help us make the
    right choices." Do you think our emotions are dependable?
    Why or why not?

    _____

    _____

# STRATEGY AND TACTICS

Former fighter pilot, Charlie Plumb says that it was the parachute packers in his life who pulled him through the loneliness and discouragement he faced during his six years as a prisoner of war during the Vietnam conflict. Charlie, now a popular seminar speaker, states that he is continually thankful for the man who carefully assembled his parachute aboard the USS *Kittyhawk* on the day his airplane was shot down over enemy territory.

But Charlie is quick to add that he is even more thankful for his cellmates in the concentration camp who carefully helped him pack his emotional, mental, and spiritual parachutes. Due to the constant help and encouragement that these extraordinary men provided, Charlie not only survived his imprisonment but also returned home a stronger person.

Soon, you will have the dubious pleasure of "flying" into an uncharted territory known as young adulthood. While you pilot through peer pressure, relating to young women, school challenges, and the other struggles of daily life, you may be "shot down" by discouragement. Your emotional health may be affected by a number of things, including your family, friends, diet, sleep patterns, and, of course, your relationship with God.

Discouragement can become a big gaping hole in your spiritual parachute. At some point, you will probably need a spiritual "parachute packer" who can encourage you as you face the enemy fire of confusion, isolation, and discouragement during your teens and into young adulthood. Use this opportunity to build a stronger relationship with your father. You can also ask your dad or pastor to identify men who could encourage you during your teenage years. Remember, they've been there, so they know what it's like to be shot down, to regroup, and then to take off again.

1a. List those people who are emotional and spiritual "parachute packers" in your life.

_____

_____

1b. How do these people support you?

_____

_____

## The Power of Hope

A few years ago, scientists conducted an experiment on hope. They took a common rat and put it into a large bowl of water. Then they watched as the rat swam around the edge of the bowl for days, staying afloat and trying to find a way to get out.

Then the scientists started the second phase of the study. They removed the first rat and put another rat into the same bowl of water, but this time they turned off all the lights in the room. Left to swim in total darkness, the second rat drowned in only a few hours, greatly surprising the scientists. Why did this rat die so quickly? The scientists concluded that it simply gave up hope. Without visual contact, the second rat had no vision of the outside world—and thus had lost all hope of survival.

Can you identify with the second rat? Have you ever felt as if you were swimming for your life in a dark bowl full of peer pressure, challenging relationships, and stressful activities? As if you could barely keep your head above water? If so, you're not alone. Many people face the darkness of discouragement.

2. List some of the possible characteristics of a discouraged person.

    1. _____

    2. _____

    3. _____

    4. _____

    5. _____

3. List some things that you think would cause someone to feel discouraged.

    1. _____

    2. _____

    3. _____

    4. _____

    5. _____

*Victory belongs to the most persevering.*

Napoleon

Many things can cause us to feel discouraged and cause us to start going downhill emotionally. The more we get discouraged and lose hope, the farther down we go. Let's look at several categories of downhills that can cause discouragement.

## Category 1: Health Downhills

▲ **Lack of sleep.** Former President Teddy Roosevelt said, "Fatigue makes cowards of us all." If we don't get enough sleep, we can become irritable and start to "cycle down."

▲ **Bad diet.** Too much sugar, caffeine, and fat can wreak havoc on our minds and our emotional stability.

▲ **Lack of exercise.** When we exercise, blood pumps oxygen into our blood and sends hormones called endorphins through our bodies to make us feel alert and energetic. When we spend too much time being a couch potato, we feel and act like sedated slugs.

## Category 2: Head Downhills

▲ **Criticism from peers.** Overly critical people can have a negative effect on our attitudes and actions.

▲ **"Successful" failure.** We can become discouraged when we fail at doing the right things, like trying our best but still losing the game.

▲ **Stress.** Too much activity makes us feel like we're under the pile and unable to dig out.

## Category 3: Heart Downhills

▲ **Unresolved conflict.** If we haven't reconnected with friends or family after an argument, we will experience a lack of closure until the problem is resolved.

▲ **"Unsuccessful" failure.** When we make a bad choice and disobey God (sin), we will feel miserable.

▲ **Unconfessed sin.** When we don't acknowledge to God that we have sinned and ask His forgiveness, guilt and discouragement will follow.

*A real leader faces the music, even when he doesn't like the tune.*

Unknown

Teknon's discouragement related to all three of these categories. He was tired and hungry. He had unresolved conflict with Pary. In addition, Magos had confused him with criticism of the CHAMPION principles, causing him to doubt his beliefs and to have a bad attitude toward Pneuma and their mission. All of these circumstances prompted him to lose hope and start riding the downhill of discouragement.

4. How might Teknon have avoided becoming discouraged?

_____

_____

5. What kind of things get you down emotionally or spiritually?

_____

_____

_____

6. Is there anything bothering you that you need to discuss with God? If so, what do plan to do?

_____

_____

_____

There's a lot you can do to dodge discouragement. To avoid the health downhills, you need to eat right, get enough sleep, and get on a regular exercise program. *To avoid the head downhills,* you should try not to spend too much time with negative people. You should also recover when you have an "unsuccessful" failure and prioritize your time by involving yourself in only a few activities at a time.

*As for avoiding the heart downhills*, you should make sure that you are doing what you can to clear up unresolved arguments with others. Most importantly, you need to remember the importance of staying in communication with Jesus Christ. If you have unconfessed sin in your life, the phone lines are cut between you and God. You need to remember how to reconnect those communication lines through confession and turning away from your sin and toward God (repentance).

7a. Remember 1 John 1:9? What does that verse say we need to do if we have disobeyed God?

_____

_____

7b. What does God promise to do in return?

_____

_____

The longer we ride the downhill of discouragement, the more we take our eyes off the One who can help us. Soon, we start losing hope and forgetting about the big picture. God doesn't want us to become discouraged.

8. You looked at Hebrews 12:1-2 in an earlier session. Look at it again, but this time focus on the first part of verse 2: "fixing our eyes on Jesus, the author and perfecter of faith ... " These verses talk about how we run the race of life that God has marked out for us and how we run to win. What is the big key to success that you find in verse 2?

_____

_____

_____

_____

9a. According to John 10:10, what kind of life does He want us to live?

_____

_____

_____

9b. What does the concept of abundant life or life lived to the full mean to you?

_____

_____

_____

_____

God wants each of us to live a meaningful, significant, maximum kind of life. He understands when you become discouraged, but He also knows that you don't have to stay that way. Take the right steps to get off of the downhill, and start riding the Abundant Life Express transport that God has for you!

## The Main Things I learned in this Champion Session are:

_____

_____

_____

_____

_____

## CHAMPION
### Sheet of Deeds

Go to the CHAMPION Sheet of Deeds on page 9 and write down **one thing you will begin to do** before the next session (and beyond) to apply the main things you learned in session 12.

# Your Mission

Complete your mission and CHAMPION Session Prep before you meet for session 13.

## Power Verse: 1 Corinthians 15:57–58

**Date memorized:** _____

## Critical Maneuver

This will reinforce what you learned in this session. Obtain your maneuver instructions from your father.

## CHAMPION Sheet of Deeds

Begin to apply your action point from your Sheet of Deeds.

## CHAMPION Session Prep

Reread episode 13 of *Teknon and the CHAMPION Warriors*, and then complete the questions in session 13 in your *Mission Guide* on your own. **Our next CHAMPION Session will be:**

Date: _____

Time: _____

Place: _____

COURAGE • HONOR • ATTITUDE • MENTAL TOUGHNESS • PURITY • INTEGRITY • OWNERSHIP • NAVIGATION

# SESSION 13:
# A JOB TO FINSIH

## CHAMPION Characteristics
**Mental Toughness and Navigation**

POWER VERSE: PHILIPPIANS 3:13B-14

*Forgetting what lies behind and reaching forward to what lies ahead,
I press on toward the goal for the prize of the upward call of God in
Christ Jesus.*

# Discussion Topics

**Choosing to focus on the mission**
**Learning to persevere even in difficult circumstances**
**Connecting with God and drawing on His power**

# Mission Debrief

1. Discuss your mission from session 12. What did you learn from your maneuver? How is what you've learned affecting your attitude or behavior?

   _____

   _____

2. Did you start applying your new action point from your Sheet of Deeds? If so, what have you learned? If not, when do you plan to get started?

   _____

   _____

3. Recite your power verse (1 Corinthians 15:57-58) from session 12.

4. In our last session, we discussed the topic of discouragement. Have you dealt with any discouragement this week? If so, how did you handle it? If not, what helped you to avoid feeling discouraged?

   _____

   _____

   _____

5. Recite the CHAMPION Warrior Creed (see page 5).

# RECONNAISSANCE

1. Review the Map of the Mission on page 8 and determine the team's location in episode 13.

2. Review the CHAMPION definition of **Mental Toughness**.

_____

_____

_____

3. Why did Teknon decide to complete the mission on his own after he defeated the amacho?

_____

_____

4. Why do you think Teknon decided to talk with Pneuma?

_____

_____

_____

5. How did Teknon make the Hoplon fly?

_____

_____

Teknon really learned to focus in this episode, didn't he? He focused in order to get back on the track of completing his mission. Did you notice how much more confident Teknon became after using his training to defeat the amacho and Rhegma? Did you notice his resolve and inner strength after he finally connected with Pneuma on a personal level?

# STRATEGY AND TACTICS

## THE POWER OF FOCUS

In the early 1900s, the United States needed a capable athlete to compete in the pentathlon, the most difficult track-and-field event of the fifth Olympiad. After much debate, the Olympic committee chose an unlikely candidate for an unlikely reason. The competitor they chose was a young army lieutenant who had displayed marginal competence in only one of the five events needed to win the pentathlon. What he lacked in ability, however, he made up with intensity. He was chosen to compete because of his determination and his focus.

He had one month to prepare for the event. During that short period of time, the focused army officer trained with unbridled passion. He forced his body to perform far beyond its normal limitations. He made it his mission to represent his country in an admirable fashion. Amazingly, he almost won a medal competing against the greatest athletes in the world. The name of the young lieutenant was George S. Patton, future four-star general of the American Armed Forces. He later became famous for his focus and determination as the leader of the Third Army that helped to defeat Hitler during World War II.

1. Are you able to focus so that you can complete a task even under stressful conditions? Would you say you are strong or need to improve a little, or need to improve a lot? Why do you say that?

_____

_____

## A MARK OF MATURITY

Pastor and author Dr. Joel Hunter says that one of the most telling marks of maturity in a person is his ability to focus on the completion of a worthy task. The ability to focus is becoming a lost art for many young people today. For the most part, our fast-

*Nobody who ever gave his best regretted it.*

George Halas

paced, entertainment-obsessed society does not see the need nor are they equipped to develop this important character trait.

Three primary things can disrupt our focus as we attempt to accomplish worthwhile objectives:

1. **Complications.** These are the problems and obstacles that come our way.

2. **Criticism.** Negative and severe judgments can come from other people or from ourselves. Criticism is an occupational hazard for a person who sets high standards for himself.

3. **Circumstances.** Usually these focus-busters come in the form of opposition against a worthwhile objective.

In the movie "October Sky," high school student Homer Hickam gazed up with amazement into a clear West Virginia night. His eyes were fixed on *Sputnik I*, the world's first orbiting satellite that was shooting across the atmosphere at 17,000 miles per hour. At that moment, he made a decision that would affect the rest of his life. He decided to build rockets.

The idea seemed impossible to everyone who knew him. Homer grew up in a small coal-mining town in which most men spent long working days a hundred feet below the earth's surface. Homer and his friends were expected to follow the same career path into the mines as soon as they graduated from high school. But Homer had a different set of dreams to pursue.

Homer and his three companions decided to build a miniature rocket in the hope of winning the national science fair. They dedicated themselves to learning physics, math, and chemistry. Step by step, enduring failure after failure, Homer and his friends moved closer to their goal. In 1957, against incredible odds, the "Rocket Boys," as they were later called, came in first place in the national science fair and went on to achieve what they wanted most. They all continued to work hard and graduated from college.

What was so special about the Rocket Boys? Why did they succeed in achieving their dreams—overcoming all the obstacles that stopped others? It's because they took responsibility to do what they could do, and they focused on completing their objectives under very difficult conditions.

The Rocket Boys studied, worked hard, and never took their focus off of their objective. That's why Homer Hickam went on to train astronauts for NASA.

2. Look up the word "focus" in the dictionary. How would you define focus in your own words?

_____

_____

_____

When a person can maintain his concentration and direct his efforts long enough to complete an important task regardless of the obstacles, he is revealing a mature mark of manhood. He's acting like a CHAMPION by doing all he can within his own CHAMPION's Ring and trusting God for the results.

## Remembering the Lion and the Bear

The Bible tells about a young man who also focused in order to complete his mission under difficult conditions. His name was David and his "super-sized" mission was defeating a giant named Goliath.

Read 1 Samuel 17:1-54

3a. Describe Goliath (verses 4-11 and 43-44).

_____

_____

_____

_____

3b. How did David view Goliath (verse 26 and 46)?

_____

_____

3c. Why did David believe that he could defeat Goliath
(verses 34-37 and 47)?

_____

_____

3d. Why did David refuse to wear King Saul's armor (verses 38-
40)?

_____

_____

3e. According to 1 Samuel 17:45-47, how did David feel about
completing his mission?  Circle the number on the following
scale that best describes his level of confidence.

     0    1    2    3    4    5    6    7    8    9    10

Very Worried                              Very Confident

3f. What did David use to defeat Goliath (verses 40 and 47-50)?

_____

_____

_____

David was willing to face Goliath because he—a shepherd
boy—remembered how God had delivered him from the lion and
the bear in the fields of Israel.  David knew that God was watching over him and protecting him.

Do you realize that God is watching over you 24/7 (24 hours a day, 7 days a week) to protect you? Psalm 121:7 gives you a great promise: "The Lord will protect you from all evil; He will keep your soul."

## How to Focus

Let's use David's example to discover some practical steps you can use to focus on completing important missions in your life.

- **Target your objective.** David targeted Goliath as the adversary he had to defeat for God and his country.
- **Train yourself for the mission.** David trained himself by conditioning both physically and spiritually during his time as a shepherd.
- **Think of the resources** you will need to complete the mission. David carefully chose his method and the tools he needed to ensure Goliath's defeat.
- **Trust that God will use and empower you** to complete any mission that He has given you. David acknowledged at an early age that his strength came from the Lord.
- **Thank God** for His faithful commitment to provide for you so that you can complete the mission. It is very important to remember how God has been faithful to you in the past. David expressed his gratitude to God for delivering him from the lion and the bear and then from Goliath.
- **Take action to complete your mission.** David acted upon his trust in God by stepping onto the battlefield. Once he made the first step to confront Goliath, there was no turning back. The Bible says that David actually charged toward Goliath on the battlefield.

It's easy to become distracted from doing the important things in our lives. Sometimes even good things can prevent us from doing the best things—those things that will make the greatest long-term impact. For example, too many basketball games or too much time with friends might prevent us from spending time reading the Bible or finishing our homework.

To become a CHAMPION, you must learn to prioritize your objectives wisely. Then you must focus your mind, your time, and your resources to complete the most important objectives before moving on to the other ones. It won't be easy. But when

*The will to win is important, but the will to prepare is vital.*

Joe Paterno

you look at guys like David, or Homer Hickam, you can see the benefits of learning how to focus.

4. What if you don't want to complete an important objective? How do you get it done if you just don't feel like it?

_____

_____

Sometimes you need to have the "want to" when it comes to completing a worthy objective. Sometimes, however, God directs you to achieve an important objective that is not fun or pleasant. If maturity can be identified by your ability to focus, then you show your level of maturity by your willingness to trust God, even through a task that offers little enjoyment through the process of completion.

5a. Which important objectives do you have that you find pretty easy to accomplish?

_____

_____

5b. Which ones are tough and demand all the focus you can muster in order to get them done?

_____

_____

5c. In what ways might God be able to help you face—and achieve—difficult objectives in your life?

_____

_____

_____

_____

*The greatest honor we can give Almighty God is to live gladly because of the knowledge of His love.*

Julian of Norwich

## The Main Things I learned in this Champion Session are:

_____

_____

_____

_____

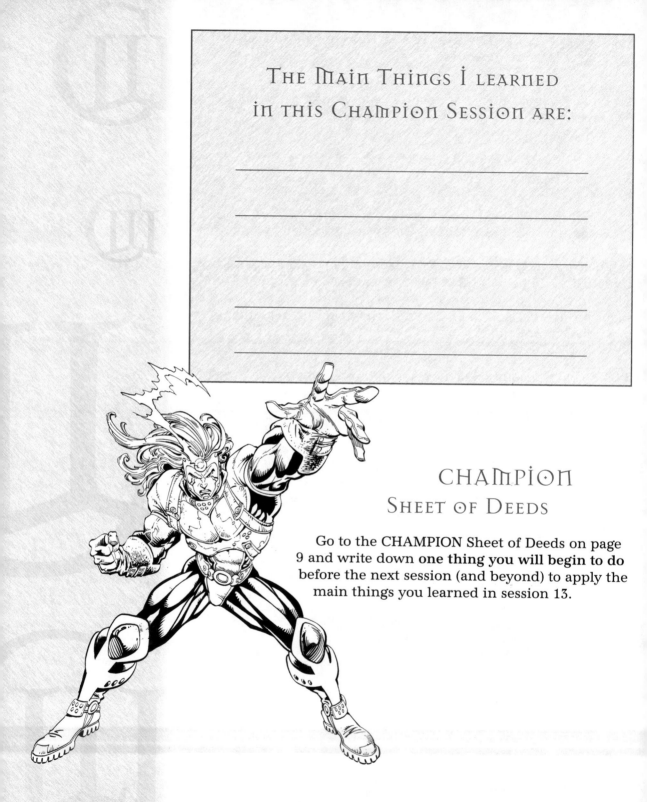

## CHAMPION
### Sheet of Deeds

Go to the **CHAMPION** Sheet of Deeds on page 9 and write down **one thing you will begin to do** before the next session (and beyond) to apply the main things you learned in session 13.

# Your Mission

Complete your mission and CHAMPION Session Prep before you meet for session14.

## Power Verse: Philippians 3:13b-14

**Date memorized:** _____

## Critical Maneuver

This will reinforce what you learned today. Obtain your maneuver instructions from your father.

## CHAMPION Sheet of Deeds

Begin to apply your action point from your Sheet of Deeds.

## CHAMPION Sesison Prep

Reread episode 14 of *Teknon and the CHAMPION Warriors*, and then complete the questions in session 14 in your *Mission Guide* on your own. **Our next CHAMPION Session will be:**

DATE:

_____

TIME:

_____

PLACE:

_____

COURAGE • HONOR • ATTITUDE • MENTAL TOUGHNESS • PURITY • INTEGRITY • OWNERSHIP • NAVIGATION

# SESSION 14:
# BACK TO BACK

## CHAMPION Characteristics

### Integrity and Attitude

POWER VERSE: PSALM 139:14

*I give thanks to You [Lord], for I am fearfully and wonderfully made; wonderful are Your works, and my soul knows it very well.*

# Discussion Topics

**Embracing the strengths and weaknesses of other people**
**Understanding my own unique bent and value to God's team**
**Harnessing the power of a diverse team to complete a mission**

# Mission Debrief

1. Discuss your mission from session 13. What did you learn from your maneuver? How is what you've learned affecting your thinking or behavior?

_____

2a. As you approach the end of your CHAMPION Training, which of your action points have you been applying from your Sheet of Deeds?

_____

_____

2b. Which of your action points have been difficult for you to apply?

_____

_____

_____

It will be important for you to put even greater focus on continuing to apply all of your action points after your CHAMPION Training is complete. Over the next few years, you will have the opportunity to use your action points to develop powerful habits that will advance your development toward courageous manhood. Don't stop the process! Remember what you have learned and continue the process of growth.

3. Recite your power verse (Philippians 3:13b-14) from session 13.

4. Is there an important objective or task that you need to complete? Look again at David's example and the six T's from session 13. Which of these will help you to focus so you can accomplish your objective? Circle them.

- ▲ Target your objective
- ▲ Train yourself for the mission
- ▲ Think of the resources you will need
- ▲ Trust that God will use and empower you
- ▲ Thank God
- ▲ Take action

5. Recite the CHAMPION Warrior Creed (see page 5).

# RECONNAISSANCE

1. Review the Map of the Mission on page 8 and determine the team's location in episode 14. They have finally achieved their objective of retrieving the Logos and defeating Magos! But success required tremendous team effort, a great deal of character, and dependence on Pneuma.

2. Review the CHAMPION definitions of **Integrity** and **Attitude**.

_____

_____

_____

_____

_____

_____

3. Why do you think Kratos waited so long to let Teknon use his Hoplon?

_____

_____

Tor explained to Teknon what it means to own the mission: "You gained the head knowledge about becoming a CHAMPION, but not the conviction of heart. For that, you had to face the possibility that no one else would retrieve the Logos unless you stepped in. When you did, the mission not only belonged to us, but to you as well."

4a. What do you think it means to "own" a mission? Is being God's CHAMPION more head knowledge for you or have you been gripped by conviction of the heart? Be honest.

4b. Do you believe God has a mission for you to own? What do you think that mission might be?

---

## Optional Questions

5a. Dolios transformed himself into Teknon's greatest fear in order to defeat him. What was Teknon's greatest fear?

_____

5b. Why do you think this was Teknon's greatest fear?

_____

_____

6. How did Teknon defeat Dolios?

_____

_____

---

*Logos* is the Greek term that means "the word." Teknon, his father, and the CHAMPION Warriors risked their lives to retrieve the Logos because of its importance to the people of Basileia. *Logos* is used in the Bible to refer to thoughts and expressions of God Himself delivered in spoken or written form to us. Jesus is also called the Logos because He is the ultimate expression of God's message to man.

7. Why is God's Word, the Bible, so important to us?

_____

_____

_____

8. Tor said, "There is great power in a team." What do you think he meant by that?

_____

_____

_____

9. Kratos instructed the warriors to "watch each other's backs." Why is it important for us to watch out for each other?

_____

_____

_____

Please fill in this chart.

Jot down five words you
think describe **Tor**:

1. _____
2. _____
3. _____
4. _____
5. _____

Jot down five words you
think describe **Epps**:

1. _____
2. _____
3. _____
4. _____
5. _____

Jot down five words you
think describe **Arti**:

1. _____
2. _____
3. _____
4. _____
5. _____

Jot down five words you
think describe **Matty**:

1. _____
2. _____
3. _____
4. _____
5. _____

# STRATEGY AND TACTICS

## DIFFERENT IS DYNAMIC

It's no secret that we all have different "bents." You may like to be the point person, positioning yourself in front of the group as the leader. Or maybe you like to be in the background keeping track of details and helping get things done. Maybe you're a natural salesman: motivating, promoting, and trying to present yourself well in the process.

Does it bother you that you're not the life of the party? Do you wish that you could make friends easier? Does it bother you that you're a cautious person or don't feel comfortable leading?

The point is this: it takes different types of players to make a great team. God uniquely designed each one of us with different strengths and weaknesses. And it's a good thing that everybody isn't alike. What would the world be like if everybody was a CEO ... or an engineer ... or a salesperson ... or a farmer ... or a public speaker?! In God's plan, different is dynamic. Your unique differences provide a dynamic contribution to the mission God has for His team here on earth. To accomplish an important mission, it takes people with different bents and strengths that can fill in each other's gaps and accomplish more as a synchronized unit than any one person could accomplish alone. Be yourself and bring your unique strengths to your family, your church, or whatever team you are a part of—and make it more dynamic!

*Coming together is a beginning; keeping together is progress; working together is success.*

Henry Ford

### HOW ARE YOU BENT?

1. What do you like best about yourself? What do other people seem to like about you?

_____

_____

_____

_____

2. Describe yourself: _____

_____

&#9650; Are you organized?

&#9650; Are you the life of the party?

&#9650; Do you like to be in charge?

&#9650; Are you a loyal and dedicated friend?

Have you ever considered how unique and important your personal traits are in accomplishing God's plan here on earth? Did you know that God designed you specifically with His perfect plan in mind?

3a. How well does God know you? (Read Psalm 139: 1-12.) What does He know about you?

_____

_____

_____

3b. According to Psalm 139, who created you?

_____

_____

3c. Describe what Psalm 139: 14-18 reveals about your design and uniqueness in God's eyes.

_____

_____

_____

Do you think God makes mistakes? Well, He's God and He doesn't! And according to Psalm 139, God made you just the way you are. And because He made you just the way you are, you are fearfully and wonderfully made in His view! Learn to appreciate who you are and find where you fit on the T-E-A-M.

*Let us not give up meeting together, as some are in the habit of doing, but let us encourage one another—and all the more as you see the Day approaching.*

**Hebrews 10:25 (NIV)**

&#10070; Teknon and the Champion Warriors &#10070;

# WHERE DO YOU FIT ON THE T-E-A-M?

Complete the following steps to assess your bent and find out where you fit:

Step 1: Under each letter category of the T-E-A-M chart, circle every word or phrase that describes a *consistent* character trait or behavior that you exhibit as you interact *within your family.*

Step 2: Total the number of items you circled in each letter category and write the total in the box at the bottom of each category.

Step 3: Plot the totals from each box on the graph entitled "What's My Bent?" on the next page. Put an "X" on each arrow scale to indicate your score for that category.

Step 4: Discuss your results.

## T

demanding   adventurous

dominant   strong-willed

decisive

task-oriented

authoritative   wants the bottom line

likes challenge   insensitive   fearless

risk taker

wants choices   competitive   problem solver

confident

likes direct answers   firm   controlling

likes freedom from control   "T" TOTAL [ ]

## E

tolerant   friendships are very important

good listener

peacemaker   wants to be liked

pleasant or likeable   passive   careful

likes security

sensitive   nurturing

avoids confrontation   likes established work patterns   patient

indecisive   thoughtful

adaptable   calm

wants to please

people-oriented   "E" TOTAL [ ]

## A

precise   correct

scheduled   calculating

consistent   likes "to do" lists

accurate   competent

analytical   cautious   likes Daytimers™ or electronic organizers

perfectionist   likes support from others   detailed

organized   discerning

predictable   likes defined tasks

practical

factual   "A" TOTAL [ ]

## M

comes up with ideas   impressive

likes to look good

very verbal

comic   inspiring

enthusiastic

optimistic   prideful

influencer   promoter/marketer   enjoys change

motivator

fun   good mixer in crowds   spontaneous

energetic   likes variety   enjoys popularity

visionary (sees the big picture)   "M" TOTAL [ ]

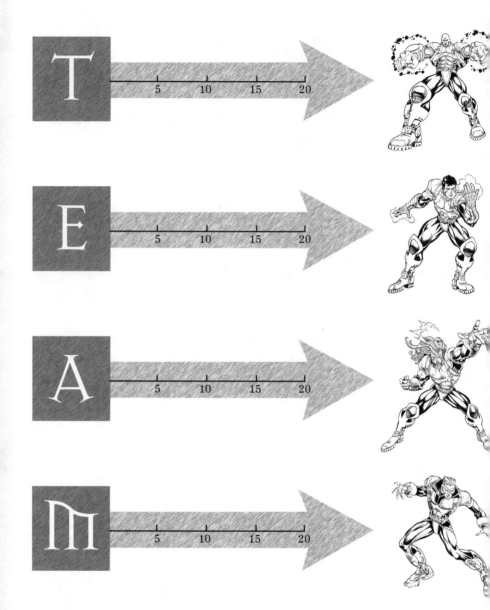

Based on your ratings, you probably notice that you identified with one of the Warriors more than the others. There's a reason for that. Even though we each have mix of traits, God created us with specific bents. For instance, if you are a strong A like Arti, you don't have to worry if you're not the one who makes everybody laugh like a strong M like Matty. As a strong A, you bring value to the team in other ways, such as your ability to get tasks done completely.

If you are a strong E like Epps, you offer a great deal to the team because of your ability to help calm things down and be a peacemaker. You may admire the leadership skills of a strong T like Tor, but it shouldn't bother you that don't always want to be in charge.

**The bottom line:** God doesn't want a team made up of clones. God blessed you with a uniquely crafted design for His special purpose in your life. Enjoy the design He gave you and use it to be an integral part of God's team. God wants you on His TEAM—and so do your family and your church!

4. After completing your T-E-A-M assessment, what do you see as some of your strengths?

_____

_____

_____

_____

*Stop comparing. Enjoy being you! There's plenty of room in the forest.*

Chuck Swindoll

5. Are there strengths or skills that you wish you had? If so, why?

_____

_____

_____

_____

_____

_____

# The Main Things I learned in this Champion Session are:

_____

_____

_____

_____

_____

## CHAMPION
### Sheet of Deeds

Go to the CHAMPION Sheet of
Deeds on page 9 and write down **one
thing you will begin to do** before
the next session (and beyond) to
apply the main things you
learned in session 14.

# Your Mission

Complete your mission and CHAMPION Session Prep before you meet for session 15.

## POWER VERSE: PSALM 139:14

**Date memorized:** _____

## CRITICAL MANEUVER

This will reinforce what you learned today. Obtain your maneuver instructions from your father.

## CHAMPION SHEET OF DEEDS

Begin to apply your action point from your Sheet of Deeds.

## CHAMPION SESSION PREP

Reread episode 15 of *Teknon and the CHAMPION Warriors*, and then complete the questions in session 15 in your *Mission Guide* on your own. **Our next CHAMPION Session will be:**

DATE:

TIME:

PLACE:

COURAGE • HONOR • ATTITUDE • MENTAL TOUGHNESS • PURITY • INTEGRITY • OWNERSHIP • NAVIGATION

# SESSION 15:
# CELEBRATION

## CHAMPION Characteristics
### Navigation and Ownership

POWER VERSE: 2 TIMOTHY 4:7–8A

*I have fought the good fight, I have finished the course, I have kept the faith; in the future there is laid up for me the crown of righteousness.*

# Discussion Topics

**Charting your course and accepting your mission**
**Earning your "wings" so you can begin to fly on your own**
**Celebrating victories and giving glory to God**

# Mission Debrief

1.  Discuss your mission from session 14. What did you learn from your maneuver? How has your attitude or behavior changed as a result of your maneuver?

    _____

2.  One final reminder about your Sheet of Deeds: If you continue to apply all of your action points, it will truly help you to grow toward courageous manhood. Select one of your action points that you will focus on as a priority over the coming weeks. Write it here and put a star by it on your Sheet of Deeds.

    _____

3.  Recite your power verse (Psalm 139:14) from session 14.

4.  Which of the four mentors do you most resemble in temperament? Who came in second on your list? List what you believe to be three of your greatest strengths from the list of temperament traits.

    _____

    _____

5.  Recite the CHAMPION Warrior Creed (see page 5).

1. Look again at the Map of the Mission, pause at each location in Teknon's quest, and remember what he learned. Then, review the key things you have learned on your quest for truth. Highlight three important lessons you have learned.

_____

_____

_____

_____

2. Review the CHAMPION definition of **Ownership**.

_____

_____

3. Why do you think Kratos took Teknon's shield back from him?

_____

_____

4. Why do you think Kratos returned Teknon's shield to him during the celebration?

_____

_____

_____

*Kratos* is a Greek word that means "power and strength." *Teknon* means "child" or "youth." During the CHAMPION Training, you have seen how much you should draw from your dad's strength of character and example. Take note that if you also strive to know God and draw on His power, as Teknon did with Pneuma, you will move from childhood toward becoming a young man of character and courage.

5. What did Kratos say to the group about Teknon during the ceremony?

_____

_____

6. Why do you think it was important for the team to celebrate after its victory on Kairos?

_____

_____

7. Why do you think it was important for Kratos to acknowledge Teknon as a young man to his friends and family?

_____

_____

8. What is the team's continuing mission?

_____

_____

_____

_____

# Strategy and Tactics

## Earning Your Wings

One of the richest and most significant traditions in our country's history is the awarding of a military pilot's "wings." When a pilot has completed his rigorous training, he is invited to a ceremony and presented with a symbol of the rank, skill, and responsibility that he has earned. When he receives his wings, he is authorized to sit behind the stick of his airplane and fly missions in the service of his country.

But just because he is awarded his wings, a pilot does not stop training. He knows that he must spend his career logging flight time, learning, training, and growing in his knowledge and piloting skills. He wants to become the best pilot that he can be.

Now that you have completed your CHAMPION Training, it's time for you to receive your "wings" and begin the flight into young manhood.

## Accept the Challenge

Life was different in the mid-1800s. More than a hundred years ago, Native Americans roamed the plains and mountains of the United States. In those days, teenagers became men almost overnight. Young Indian men knew that when they reached a certain age, they were expected to provide and care for a family. They were also expected to join the rest of the warriors from their tribe in battle.

At what age would you be ready to assume responsibility for a family or be willing to fight an enemy to protect your homeland? If you were a Native American during the mid–1800s, you would have been about 14 years old.

But life is quite different for many teens today. Instead of using their talents and resources to set worthy goals and accomplish great tasks when they're young, they usually settle for trying to get homework done in time to watch TV or get on the Internet. They expect too little of themselves.

*Throughout the centuries, there were men who took the first steps down new roads armed with nothing but their own vision.*

Ayn Rand

You may not be in this camp, especially after finishing your CHAMPION Training. There are teens who are making a difference in their families and communities. They remember that God is the ultimate source of their talents and resources. They are thankful for what they have and want to be good stewards. They are taking responsibility—helping their parents, working hard at school, reaching out to other people, learning what friendship is all about, setting the right boundaries, and so on. These young people have learned to set high standards for themselves and they are meeting important objectives in life. They seek to know God better and to share Him with others. But remember, there's always room for growth.

An important key to living as a courageous man is to recognize the source of your talents and resources. Once you really grasp Who gave you your abilities and why He gave them to you, your life will never be the same. Let's look at a man in the Bible who learned about the power of God and how God could use him to accomplish mighty things for His people.

## WHAT ARE YOU WAITING FOR?

Moses, an Israelite, was adopted by Pharaoh's daughter and raised as a prince in Egypt. But he was enraged about the treatment of his people, who were enslaved and pushed down under the heavy hand of the Egyptians. Initially, he tried to accomplish the mission of freeing his people in his own strength—he killed an Egyptian and had to run away.

Before Moses could become camp counselor to almost seven million people, the leader of the entire nation of Israel, he had to be humbled. He needed time to reflect, to think about who he was, and to learn to depend on God. So God allowed him to shepherd sheep for 40 years in the hills of what became the nation of Israel.

1. According to Exodus 3:1-10, what did God use to get Moses' attention? What did He want Moses to do?

_____

_____

_____

2. When Moses was afraid to carry out the mission God had given him, what did God promise to do for Moses (see Exodus 3:12-21)?

_____

_____

As God continued to speak to Moses out of the burning bush to reveal His plan to deliver the Israelites from Egypt, He told Moses to do something very puzzling.

Read Exodus 4:1-5.

3a. What was in Moses' hand?

_____

3b. What did God tell Moses to do with it the staff?

_____

3c. What did God tell Moses to do next?

_____

3d. Why do you think God told Moses to do these things (see verse 5)?

_____

_____

After 40 years of being a shepherd, God told Moses to lay down his staff. A staff was the most important tool a shepherd owned. It was an instrument he used to guide his sheep through the mountains and it was a weapon he used to ward off wild animals that tried to attack the flock. A shepherd valued his staff even more than Tiger Woods values his driver. Over time, Moses' staff had become like an extension of his arm. He seldom went anywhere without it. The staff was also Moses' security. After all, he had been comfortably hiding out in the wilderness for 40 years. God was asking Moses to take a giant step out his comfort zone.

When God asked Moses to lay down his staff, it was like Kratos asking Teknon to return his shield. Moses may not have understood God's reasoning, but he obeyed anyway. God showed Moses the miracles He would perform through the staff and explained that through these miracles the Israelites would know that He had truly appeared to Moses. When God returned the newly designed shepherd's tool to Moses, it was no longer the staff of Moses. It was now the staff of God! The staff became God's instrument to accomplish His mission through Moses.

5.  Review the CHAMPION definition of **Navigation**.

_____

_____

Have you grasped through your training that God has a mission for each of us? Do you realize that He has given you the talents and resources you need to accomplish the mission He has for you? When you use your talents for God, and depend on His power, you are exercising good stewardship. You are becoming God's instrument on earth to accomplish His mission.

So what are you waiting for? Get involved in God's mission as a CHAMPION. Trust Him to accomplish the impossible in and through you (that's within God's Ring of Responsibility), but make sure that you're taking responsibility to do all that you can to seek God and pursue excellence in every part of your life (that's within your CHAMPION's Ring). Shouldn't you use the abilities and assets that God has given you to accomplish His goals? God's mission will unfold for you day by day if you will commit to follow Him. It's a great adventure!

One more thing ... it's time to celebrate! You've just completed the entire CHAMPION Training adventure. You've read the episodes, answered the questions, discussed many topics with your dad, and completed the maneuvers and action points. Take time to enjoy this victory and any other victories that you've experienced during your CHAMPION Training. God wants to celebrate the wins in your life and He wants you to celebrate with Him. Thank God for what he has done and for what He will do in and through you as you live your life as a CHAMPION.

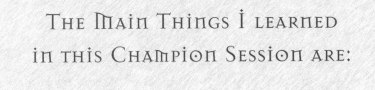

# The Main Things I learned in this Champion Session are:

_____

_____

_____

_____

*And looking at them Jesus said to them, "With people this is impossible, but with God all things are possible."*

Matthew 19:26

## CHAMPION
### Sheet of Deeds

Go to the **CHAMPION** Sheet of Deeds on page 9 and write down **one thing you will begin to do** before the next session (and beyond) to apply the main things you learned in session 15.

# Your Mission

Complete your mission before you meet for your Celebration Ceremony.

## Power Verse: 2 Timothy 4:7-8a

**Date memorized:** _____

## Critical Maneuver

This will reinforce what you learned today. Obtain your maneuver instructions from your father.

## CHAMPION Sheet of Deeds

Continue to apply your action points from your Sheet of Deeds.

## Celebration Ceremony

If your dad is planning a celebration ceremony for you, write down the specifics here.

Dad, celebrate your son's accomplishment in completing his CHAMPION Training with a ceremony! Refer to chapter 4 of your *Mentor Guide* for practical tips on putting together an effective ceremony for your son. My Celebration Ceremony will be:

Date: _____

Time: _____

Place: _____

# Congratulations on a job well done!

Nike® says it, and we buy into it. You look at the "swoosh," as Nike calls it, and the phrase comes to your mind. You hear it in commercials, you see it on the billboards, and it's plastered on millions of shirts, shoes, and shorts. Over a period of time, we come to believe it only because some well-paid marketing wizards found a creative way to sell more products. Now, why don't we say that phrase all together? Ready, one, two, three:

# Just Do It!

If only all of life were as easy as this slogan makes it sound. The truth is, life is a lot harder than selling trendy clothing. In fact, we can't "just do it" on our own when it comes to living a life in which we're unconditionally loved, eternally protected, and fully satisfied.

We need power to do that—a lot of power. Power that can only come from an all-powerful God who wants us to relate to Him on a personal level. Only those people who know Him and seek Him have access to God's unlimited power. He offers it as a free gift that we receive through faith in His Son, Jesus Christ.

God created us to have an abundant life now and for eternity. But He did not create us like androids that would automatically love and follow Him. He gave us a will and freedom to choose or eternal destination. What will you choose?

Are you 100% sure that, when you die, you are going to heaven? Why do you say that?

Mark on the following scale, how sure are you that you have a personal relationship with God, through Jesus Christ?

Not at all sure    1      2      3      4      5      Very sure

How do you know?

_____

_____

Would you like to be 100% fully sure that you have a personal relationship with God that will guarantee your passport to heaven?

_____

_____

God's power is experienced by knowing God personally and by growing in our relationship with Him. God has provided the power necessary to fulfill His purposes and to carry out His mission for our lives. God is so eager to establish a personal, loving relationship with you that He has already made all the arrangements. He is patiently and lovingly waiting for you to respond to His invitation.

The major barrier that prevents us from knowing God personally is ignorance of who God is and what he has done for us. The following four principles will help you discover how to know God personally and experience the abundant life He promised.

G OD LOVES YOU AND CREATED YOU TO KNOW H IM PERSONALLY.

### a. God loves you.

"For God so loved the world, that He gave His only begotten Son, that whoever believes in Him should not perish but have eternal life." John 3:16

### b. God wants you to know Him.

"Now this is eternal life: that they may know You, the only true God, and Jesus Christ, whom You have sent." John 17:3 (NIV)

*What prevents us from knowing God personally?*

 W E ARE SINFUL AND SEPARATED FROM G OD, SO WE CANNOT KNOW H IM PERSONALLY OR EXPERIENCE H IS LOVE AND POWER.

*(Author's Note: The word sin confuses a lot of people. The word sin comes from a Greek term that was used in archery. When archers shot at the target, the distance by which their arrow missed the bull's-eye was called sin. That distance represented the degree to which the archer missed the mark of perfection. When we miss God's mark of perfection, it's called sin too. And because of sin, there is a wall that separates us from a perfectly holy God. Through the years, people have tried many things to break through that wall. Money, power, and fame are just a few of the things people have tried. None of them have worked. We all fall short of God's perfection.)*

### a. Man is sinful.

"For all have sinned and fall short of the glory of God." Romans 3:23

### b. Man is separated.

For the wages of sin is death [spiritual separation from God]. Romans 6:23a

*How can the canyon between God and man be bridged?*

**3** Jesus Christ is the only provision for man's sin. Through Him alone we can know God personally and experience God's love.

a. God became a man through the Person of Jesus Christ.

> But the angel said to them, "Do not be afraid; for behold, I bring you good news of great joy which will be for all the people; for today in the city of David there has been born for you a Savior, who is Christ the Lord." Luke 2:10-11

b. He died in our place.

> "But God demonstrates His own love toward us in that while we were yet sinners, Christ died for us." Romans 5:8

c. He rose from the dead.

> "Christ died for our sins according to the Scriptures ... He was buried ... He was raised on the third day according to the Scriptures ... He appeared to Peter, then to the twelve. After that He appeared to more than five hundred." 1 Corinthians 15:3b-6a

d. He is the only way to God.

> "Jesus said to him, 'I am the way, and the truth, and the life; no one comes to the Father but through Me.'" John 14:6

*It is not enough to know these truths ...*

 **4** We must individually receive Jesus Christ as Savior and Lord; then we can know God personally and experience His love.

a. We must receive Christ.

> "But as many as received Him, to them He gave the right to become children of God, even to those who believe in His name." John 1:12

b. We must receive Christ through faith.

> "For by grace you have been saved through faith; and that not of yourselves, it is the gift of God; not as a result of works, so that no one may boast." Ephesians 2:8-9

c. When we receive Christ we experience a new birth (read John 3:1-8).

d. We must receive Christ by personal invitation.

> "I am the door; if anyone enters through Me, he will be saved ..." John 10:9

Receiving Christ involves turning to God from self (repentance) and trusting Christ to come into our lives to forgive us of our sins and to make us what He wants us to be. Just to agree intellectually that Jesus Christ is the Son of God and that He died on the cross for our sins is not enough. Nor is it enough to have an emotional experience. We receive Jesus Christ by faith, as an act of our will.

These two circles represent two kinds of lives:

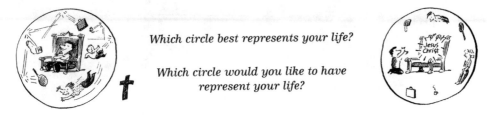

*Which circle best represents your life?*

*Which circle would you like to have represent your life?*

## You Can Receive Christ Right Now By Faith Through Prayer

God knows your heart and is not so concerned with your words as He is with the attitude of your heart. Here is a suggested life-changing prayer:

> Lord Jesus, I want to know You personally. Thank you for dying on the cross for my sins. I open the door of my life and receive You as my Savior and Lord. Thanks you for forgiving me of my sins and giving me eternal life. Take control of the throne of my life. Make me the kind of person You want me to be.
>
> If you sincerely prayed this prayer, you can know with 100% certainty that Christ is in your life and He is there to stay (Hebrews 13:5). So, you don't have to "just do it". God has already done it for you. You may or may not feel like it now, but this is the most important day of your life. To remember this major event in your life when you joined God's family, sign and date this page.

_____          _____
              *Signature*                              *Date*

## What Are the Results of Placing Your Faith in Jesus Christ?

The Bible says:

1. Jesus Christ came into your life (Colossians 1:27).

2. Your sins were forgiven (Colossians 1:14).

3. You became a child of God (John 1:12)

4. You received eternal life (John 5:24).

5. You have the power to pursue intimacy with God (Romans 5:5).

6. You began the great adventure, the mission, for which God created you (John 10:10, 2 Corinthians 5:17, and 1 Thessalonians 5:18).

# CHAMPION
# Training Adventure
# Program

For other *Teknon and the Champion Warriors* resources check out our Web site at www.familylife.com/teknon for:

▲ Character illustrations and descriptions

▲ Downloadable CHAMPION Creed and Code

▲ Downloadable sample forms

▲ New ideas for CHAMPION Training

▲ Great links and more!

# Media Evaluation Report

When using movies, audio cassettes, and books for action points, consider asking your son to write a one-page report that answers the following questions.

1. How would you summarize the movie, audio cassette, or book?

2. What is the main point of the story?

3. Who is the hero?  Who is the villain?

4. What skills or gifts did the hero rely on to succeed?

5. Do you agree with the hero's behavior and the methods he used?  If not, what would you have done in his place?

6. What CHAMPION characteristics did the hero exhibit?

7. As you think of this story, name one story or passage from the Bible that it reminds you of.

8. How do the messages in this apply to me?

9. List other special questions identified in the *Mentor Guide* for each session:

   - 

   - 

   -

# Acknowledgements

Putting together an integrated program with a fiction novel for teens, an interactive training guide, and a comprehensive how-to manual for dads has been quite a challenge. There are a number of people I wish to thank for helping me to make *Teknon and the CHAMPION Warriors* a reality.

I would like to thank Neal and Ida Jean Sapp, Sam Bartlett, Sheri and Jack McGill, Dr. Gilbert Chandler, Martin Shipman, Don Jacobs, Roger Berry, Nick and Amy Repak, Michael Hohmann, Steve Bruton, Sergio Cariello, Rick Blanchette, Donald Joy, and Stephen Sorenson for their invaluable input and encouragement.

I also appreciate the dedicated team at FamilyLife for the theological, editorial, and design direction. This team includes Jerry McCall, Blair Wright, David Sims, Bob Anderson, Anne Wooten, and Fran Taylor.

My heartfelt thanks are extended to Ben Colter who, through his hard work and creative editing expertise, has helped to transform this material into an adventurous, user-friendly training program that we hope will greatly benefit both you and your son.

I want to thank my wife, Ellen, for striving with me to raise our children with strong character and for enduring the process of developing these materials. Last, but not least, I want to acknowledge my children, Katie, Kimberly, Kyle, and especially Casey for giving me encouragement and inspiration during the creative development of the CHAMPION Training adventure program. Thanks, kids!

# Notes

## Session 6

Original source unknown for "Nasty as We Wanna Be" article.

# ABOUT THE AUTHOR

Brent Sapp is a first time writer from Orlando. When his older son, Casey, was nearing the teen years, Brent conceived a fun program that he and some friends pursued together with their sons. They called themselves CHAMPION Warriors. The program caught on in Florida and in other areas of the country. From this successful venture, Brent has adapted the key principles of a CHAMPION into a futuristic adventure novel for teen boys. He has also developed an interactive character-building program for fathers to use with their sons as a companion resource to *Teknon and the CHAMPION Warriors*.

Brent and his wife, Ellen, have four children (Casey, 16; Katie, 14; Kimberly, 12; and Kyle, 9). Brent is a graduate of Florida State University and has an MBA from Rollins College. He has worked as a medical sales representative for the past 16 years. When not representing medical and surgical equipment, Brent volunteers with Ellen to help bring the FamilyLife Marriage Conference to Orlando and also to prepare dozens of young couples for marriage each year at Northland Community Church.

# ABOUT THE ILLUSTRATOR

Sergio Cariello is the talented free-lance illustrator behind the characters of *Teknon and the CHAMPION Warriors*. He also draws such well-known icons as Superman and Batman for DC Comics. In addition, he teaches at the prestigious Joe Kubert School of Cartooning and Animation. Sergio lives in South River, N.J., with his wife, Luzia.

# Notes

# Notes

# NOTES

# Notes

# NOTES

# NOTES

# Notes

# Notes

# Notes

# Notes

# Notes

# Notes

# Notes

# NOTES

# Notes

Ron Curran's

# *INSTANT GOLF*

AND

## *THE SIMPLE SWING*

Published 1996 by Buy a Better Game.
West Chester, Ohio

***INSTANT GOLF***

Published 1996 by Buy a Better Game.
West Chester, Ohio

Copyright 1996 by W.R.Curran
All rights reserved
Published by Buy a Better Game
9042 Hollywood Court
West Chester, Ohio 45069
Manufactured in the USA
International Standard Book Number: 0-9650346-3-1

# INTRODUCTION

**T**his book is based on Ron Curran's *Instant Golf* three hour workshop.

*Instant Golf* is not a traditional golf instructional book. First, *Instant Golf* uses advanced learning techniques which go against traditional learning methods. Talk to any golfing instructor and he will tell you that you can only learn to play good golf with lessons at the range and with a great deal of practice, both on the range and on the course. He will also tell you to learn only from an expert golfer, one who has qualified as a Professional Golf Association member.

The U.S. Army once thought this way. They thought the only way they could teach pistols was to take their best marksmen and make them instructors. They also felt the only way to learn was by doing, so they put the students on the firing range for three days and let them fire as many rounds as they desired. After three days of practice, with instructors looking over there shoulders, the end result was less than half of every class qualified for pistols.

A non pistol expert challenged the Army by stating he could increase the results in less time. The Army took the challenge, and in only a day of instruction and with less than three hours of practice on the firing range, 95% of the class qualified for pistols. This approach yielded twice the results in half the time.

**W**hat was the instructor's secret? He made sure the students fully understood every aspect of shooting a pistol before they ever fired one on the range.

No, you do not need to learn by doing, i.e. trial and error. Kids learn best this way, but as you know, if you are over 30, adults learn differently from kids. This fact has escaped the golfing community because 99.9% of all teaching pros learned to play golf as children or as young adults. People who learned to play golf when their bodies were supple and when they could practice from sunup, to sundown have a hard time relating to someone over 30, whose body is no longer supple and who has limited time to practice due to adult matters like family, business, church and community. You can't learn right if you are taught wrong.

As one of these adult students, I tried their way for over 10 years. I took the lessons; I went to the golf schools; and because I traveled a great deal, I had the time to practice in the evening during day-light-saving-time hours. I had one problem however, I never seemed to get any better! On those occasions when I began to strike the ball fairly well, I would have an instructor tell me my backswing was getting too short or I wasn't shifting my weight properly.

One day the light bulb can on. The pros were trying to teach me to swing like a pro but I was simply too old to learn to swing like a pro. At that point I started to research what had worked for me and for others my age.

Once I stopped listening to the pros, both in person and in the print and video media, my handicap dropped from a 19 to an 11. When I stopped playing from the back tees and went to the front tees, my handicap went into the single digit range. I tell you this because I don't want to put myself before you as a great golfer, because I am not.

However, I am a very good teacher, and I do know something you need to know. I know what keeps most social and beginning golfers from becoming solid, respectable golfers, and I know how to get you to that solid, respectable stage in a hurry without costly lessons and without spending countless hours on the practice range.

Phrases you will see repeatedly throughout  this book!

- Knowledge does not equal learning.  Knowledge plus belief equals learning.

- If you want to swing like a pro you must learn and practice like a pro.  If you are not going to learn and practice like a pro, (and you can't)  you can't expect to swing like one.

- Golf is not a Natural Game!

- You cannot play any sport played with a ball well, including golf, without developing some sense of touch or feel.

- Short and reliable is better than long and unreliable.

- By the yard everything is hard, but by the inch anything is a cinch.

- Golf is not rocket science.

## SOLID, RESPECTABLE GOLF
and why lessons don't work!

You are about to learn to play SOLID, RESPECT-ABLE, GOLF and you are about to do it almost instantly. Even if you have never before held a golf club in your hand, you can play SOLID, RESPECT-ABLE, GOLF in three hours (without costly lessons and without spending a lot of time on the practice tee). If you have played golf before, this process will take you a little longer as you must work on breaking old habits as well as establishing new ones.

Now let's understand what I said. I did not say you will be good enough to go on the PGA tours, and I didn't say you will become a club champion. What I did say was you will play SOLID, RESPECTABLE GOLF; solid in the sense that you will be able to hit the ball solidly time after time after time; respectable in the sense of keeping the ball in play on or near the fairway.

I have never met either you nor your future playing companions, but I can tell you one important fact about each of you. As a new golfer what you fear most about going out to play golf is embarrassment. You are afraid you will embarrass yourself while on the course. This embarrassment may come by not being able to hit the ball off the tee at the first hole. If you do hit the ball, you are afraid it won't go into the air; or if it does fly in the air, you won't have the slightest idea where it might go. You are afraid the ball will end up in the rough or in the woods where everyone will be compelled to interrupt his or her game to help you hunt for your lost

7

ball. Having other people constantly looking for your lost ball, hole-after-hole, isn't only embarrassing, but it may slow the whole group down to the point where a ranger may appear and ask your group either to play faster and keep up with the group in front of your group. This, of course, leads to more embarrassment.

Rather than face such embarrassment, some people will just stay home when their business associates, friends, or family members invite them out for a round of golf. With *INSTANT GOLF*, you won't fear such embarrassment because you know you will be able to hit the ball solidly time-after-time, and you will be able to keep the ball in play on or near the fairway.

Surprising as it may seem, your playing companions will not be concerned about your score. They don't care if you shoot 90 or 120. What they want any new golfer to be able to do is to play quickly, safely and courteously.

Quickly does not mean run to your ball and hit it as fast as you can. No, what it means is to be ready to hit when it is your turn to hit, and to be able to move (advance) the ball towards the target. It is okay if you only advance the ball a short distance as long as it doesn't go astray and cause others to interrupt their game to look for your ball. Around the green, "quickly" means being able to get the ball in the cup in a few, usually two and certainly no more than three, strokes. Your playing companions certainly don't want you to play "ping pong" on the green with the cup being used as the net, that is to say, hitting the ball 20 feet past the hole on the first putt and then hitting it 20 feet past the hole on the next putt in the opposite direction.

Safety is best accomplished by always staying behind the ball when someone else is hitting the ball and always making sure no one is in your line of fire when you are hitting the ball.

Finally, courteously means keeping still and quiet while others are hitting or putting. It means replacing your divots, raking bunkers, and repairing your ball mark on the green. It means using hand gestures when you are happy or disappointed rather than shouting out loud and disturbing other players on the next green, tee, or fairway.

If you can keep the ball in play and have some sense of touch around the green then, you will be playing SOLID, RESPECTABLE, GOLF. You will be able to play quickly, safely, and courteously. You will therefore be a welcome addition to any golfing group regardless of how well they play or how high a score you shoot.

My goal is not to get you to the point where you can beat your boss, customer, or father-in-law in a game of golf. It is to get you on the course with them without embarrassing either yourself or them. The handicap system in golf will even out the differences in ability and allow for a competitive game.

## Getting Started

Okay, you are over 30 (maybe way over 30) and you want to play golf. I will tell you something either the teaching pros don't know, don't want to admit, or simply feel is in their best interest to keep from you:

"If you want to swing like a pro, you need to learn and practice like a pro."

99.9% of the pros started playing golf at a very young age, when learning was easy, when their bodies were supple and when they could practice from sunup to sundown. They learned the golf swing as one complete action rather than a series of actions i.e., the backswing, the follow-through etc., and they learned by doing, not thinking.

Adults learn differently from children. Children do and act; adults analyze and react. Since you, as an adult, can no longer learn as a child, the odds of your developing a fluid, pro-type swing are slim and none; and for every year you are over 30, slim gets even slimmer. Stated another way, if you don't already have a consistent classic pro-type swing by the time you are 30, no matter how much you practice, no matter how much you spend on lessons, the odds are stacked against you to obtain that long, graceful, powerful, classic swing you see on TV.

People, who have taken up the game of golf after the age of 30, soon discover this fact; but then they listen to their teaching pros or they read the golfing books and articles and watch instructional videos and are forever told that if they will just work hard enough, they can do it. When, not if, the student fails, it is blamed on their lack of practice or even their lack of talent; when in fact, they were given the wrong instructions, and were ask to perform tasks they were incapable of performing consistently.

The people who were and are instructing them didn't learn to play golf as adults. They learned as children, and therefore haven't the vaguest idea of what it is like to be over 30 and to endeavor to train one's body to behave in a manner completely foreign to it.

This is what Jack Nicklaus writes in his book LESSON TEE about his downswing: "My downswing actually starts before my backswing is completed. The forward action begins in my feet. As the very first move on the downswing, while my arms are still swinging up, my left heel returns to earth and I begin to push hard off the inside of my right foot, throwing weight laterally to the inside of my left foot"

How much practice will you need to get your timing down so your downswing starts before you complete your backswing?

I contend no amount of practice will allow most golfers, who started playing golf after 30, to develop such a swing.

By the way, swimming coaches will tell you the same thing. People who learn to swim as adults will never develop the same graceful swimming motion of someone who learned to swim as a child. Ballet teachers will tell you that adults who take up dancing will never flow like the adult who learned as a child.

Let me give you two stories that will illustrate my point. A father, age 35, and son, age 14, take up the game of golf together. Two years later the father is still struggling to shoot in the 90's and may still be posting scores over 100 while the son is already shooting in the 70's and is flirting with par.

Or take the case of a salesmen, who had learned the game at an early age, but had given it up as an adult. Ten years later, a customer almost forced him onto the golf course by threatening to take away his business unless he joined them in a round of golf. With borrowed clubs and sneakers rather than golf shoes, he shot a 78. When asked how he did it, he said, "It could have been a 75, but I missed some putts." For him playing golf was like riding a bike. He learned as a child how to do both and would always know how to do both.

Golfers, if you take up the game after 30 and insist on using the classic pro-type swing, you are simply playing golf's version of Russian Roulette. You might win at Russian Roulette if you play it once; but if you play it often enough, you will lose. You may get away with a classic pro-type swing for a while, but somewhere during the round the gun will go off and your high scoring holes will appear.

Does this mean you can't play a decent game of golf if you take the game up after childhood? Of course not. What is does mean, as stated in the movie Dirty Harry, "A man has got to know his limitations." Once you realize your limitation concerning the golf swing, you can begin devoting your energies to those things which will make a difference in your game and score and not waste your time and money trying to develop a picture perfect golf swing.

Just as shooting a basketball is not playing basketball (basketball is about many things like teamwork, defense, rebounding, passing, moving without the ball etc.), golf is about chipping and putting and recovery - not just about the golf swing.

Because adults learn through analyzation, they tend to get "paralysis by analysis". *Instant Golf* is designed to make what you need to do to play golf so simple that very little analysis is needed. You will then be able to do what adults do best - react!

**I**f taking lessons from a pro is a mistake, learning from a friend or family member may be even worse.

While it may be true this person is a very good golfer, the odds are he or she is not a very good teacher. Most people believe the way to teach is to impart knowledge, but knowledge does not equal learning. If it did, all we would need to do is tell our kids what to do and not to do and they would act accordingly, which of course they don't. No, knowledge plus "belief" equals learning and most friends or family members have no way of helping a new golfer establish this belief. Instead, they usually impart too much knowledge and overcorrect the student after each swing.

One woman told me she stopped counting after her husband had given her over one hundred criticisms (he called them instructions) during a round of golf. She now understands the poem, "My husband has turned into a louse, I should have known not to take golfing lessons from my spouse."

**F**inally, there are the golf schools. These schools can run from three days to seven days. These schools try to give the student a systematic (total) approach to the game of golf. They give classroom instructions, something the local pro rarely does, and they place emphasis on the short game and course management. Golfers get to practice under the eyes of an instructor at the range or practice green, and they get to put what they learned in the morning to use on the course in the afternoon. The major problems with the golf schools is their cost - from just under $1000 to over $4000. When the cost of the travel is added to these figures, you can see that Golf Schools can be dreadfully expensive.

*I*nstant *Golf* has taken the "Golf School" approach, but we have replaced the pro-type swing (with all its many moving parts) with a simple swing (with only a few moving parts). We have also added some advance teaching methods. All of this allows us to compress the learning time down from days and weeks to a few hours.

## ISLAND OF "Respectable Golfers"

Before we begin working on your game, I want you to visualize a mainland and three islands just off shore. On the mainland are the "beginning golfers". On the island, just off shore, live the "respectable golfers" (golfers who can score in the 90's and sometimes in the 80's). Since the average golf score at a public golf course on a weekend, if all the strokes were counted and all the scores were recorded, would be well above 100, these "respectable golfers" are better than the average golfers. Farther out on the second and third islands are the "very good" and the "exceptional" golfers. If "beginners "stay on the mainland long enough, they cease to be "beginners" and are referred to as "hackers", "duffers", or more humanely as "recreational" golfers or "weekend warriors".

**14**

Unfortunately, many golfers never cross over to the first island because either they, or the people instructing them, want to "leapfrog" them over the first island and onto the second island. I once heard on a radio "call in" show, a nationally known pro golfer tell a beginning golfer that the first thing he should work on is proper weight shift. Great advice for a youngster learning golf, but it is poor advise for someone over 30 who needs first to learn to hit the ball solidly and straight and concentrating on shifting his or her weight during the swing might lessen their chances of accomplishing this objective.

There once were two men of the cloth traveling a dirt trail when they came upon a stream with no bridge. The first man said, "I have great faith," and with that he proceeded to walk across the stream over to the other side as if he were walking on water. The second man said, "I too have great faith," and with that he proceeded to step on the water only to fall in up to his waist. When he reached the other side, he was totally confused. "What happened?," he asked, "My faith is as strong as yours yet, you were able to walk over the stream with ease. When I tried it, I almost drowned."

Smiling, the first clergyman replied, "It helps to know where the rocks are."

There are four "stepping stones" a beginning golfer must locate before he or she can cross over from the land of "Beginning Golfers" to the island of the "Respectable Golfers". No golfer can cross over until they

**15**

locate these rocks. As stated earlier, many golfers never find the rocks; for others it takes quite a while to locate them. *Instant Golf* knows where they are and by pointing these stepping stones out to you, you will be able to make the trip from beginning golfer to respectable golfer almost instantly.

THE FOUR STEPPING STONES OF *INSTANT GOLF*

Beginning golfers and recreational golfers make four mistakes that prevent them from moving to the next level of golf.

**1**. Golf **is not** a <u>natural game</u>.

Beginning golfers are never told or never quite understand this and therefore they do things naturally and fail.

**2**. A sense of "**Touch and Feel**" must be developed to play any game that has to do with manipulating a ball.

Many beginning golfers never realize this and even if they do, they have no way of developing Touch or Feel.

**3**. There is **no such thing** as a <u>"Hit and Lift"</u> shot in the game of golf.

Beginning golfers assume if a ball is on the ground and they want it to go into the air, they must get the clubhead under the ball in order

to get the ball to go skyward. This is simply
not true.

4. "**Short and Reliable**" is more effective than
"Long and Unreliable."

Beginning golfers mistakenly believe in order
to play golf they must take a long backswing
to hit the ball hard and far. Wrong again. Golf
is a game of effortless power, not powerful effort.

Knowledge does not equal learning! You now have
the knowledge you need to play "Solid, Respectable
Golf", but knowledge does not equal learning. In
order to learn something, there must be a "belief" or
"ownership" of the knowledge.

Let me ask you a question. When you were first
taught how to drive a car, were you told not to slam
on your brakes when driving on ice? You had the
knowledge but did you really own this principle, or
did you need to get on ice and slam on the brakes
and experience for yourself the results before you
really fully understood the importance of this information? Once you experienced the results of the
knowledge you had belief and you owned the principle. Knowledge plus belief equals learning. What *Instant Golf* will do is give you the knowledge and the
belief you need to make learning occur almost instantly.

**17**

# STEPPING STONE NUMBER ONE

GOLF IS NOT A NATURAL GAME.

**B**efore you begin this section, I want you to close your eyes and imagine you are going to hit two golf shots. For the first swing imagine you are going to hit a ball over a pond 100 yards wide using an 8 iron. On the second swing you are going to hit a golf ball two hundred yards off a tee with a driver. I know you don't know how yet, but as they say at Disney World, "Play the game." Ready, go! Now keep those pictures in your mind as we discuss GOLF IS NOT A NATURAL GAME.

**Golf is not a natural game!**
    If you want to know what to do correctly in the game of golf, try to figure out what is the natural way to do it, and then do the opposite. If golf were really a natural game, why would you need lessons of any kind? Just go out and swing the club and record your par score. Par is the score a very good golfer is supposed to make on each hole as well as for the entire course. Example: A par 3 hole while the course itself is a par 72.
    The point I need to make throughout this section is, if you wish to play solid, respectable golf in a few short hours, the first prerequisite is to force your-

self to resist the temptation to do things the natural way. *INSTANT GOLF* requires you to <u>think your way around the golf course.</u>

For years, pros who learned to play golf as youngsters, have been instructing adult beginners not to think while on the course. "Just go out and play", they advise. This is the way they learned, so surely it is good advice for their students. Unfortunately, for the pro and the student, adults are pondering beings and analyzation is as much a part of how an adult learns as breathing is to life. *Instant Golf* recognizes this fact and implores you to use it to your advantage. What follows is designed to get you to own or believe this because without this principle you can't locate the other stones.

When I ask you to visualize hitting a ball 100 yards over water, did you try to hit under the ball and try to lift it into the air? If you did, you did the natural thing. It is a natural act to think you need to help the ball into the air, but it is wrong.

The first shot only had to go 100 yards over water. The second shot needed to go 200 yards.

How much faster or how much harder did you swing the driver in order to get the ball to travel twice as far? Did you try to swing twice as fast? It is only logical to assume you need twice the speed or power to hit a ball twice as far, isn't it? The truth is, golf is not a natural game, and while it might seem logical you would need to swing harder to get the ball to go farther, it just ain't so. The speed of the swing should always be the same no matter what club you have in your hand, or how far you want the ball to go. If this statement seems totally illogical to you, please don't feel alone because golf is not a natural game. Almost every golfer who has picked up a golf club has a hard time with this fact until it has been proven to him or her.

From the wedge back to the fairway clubs, <u>all clubs must be swung at the same controlled rate of speed</u>. Some of the most intelligent people I know claim it was impossible for me to teach them to hit a fairway wood successfully. I always take the challenge and ask them to bring a pitching wedge and a fairway wood to the practice range. I first have them hit five or six successful pitching wedge shots. When they feel they are in a good rhythm, I ask them to switch to the fairway wood and to think like they are still hitting the pitching wedge. Eight out of ten people will speed up the swing of the fairway wood. When asked why they did so, they aren't able to explain it. The secret may be to think swing even slower with the fairway wood, but we will get to that later. For now, however, your task is to know that it is perfectly natural to want to swing the woods faster than the irons, but once again, all together now; **"GOLF IS NOT A NATURAL GAME"**.

**W**hen you were asked to visualize hitting the ball 200 yards, how tightly were you gripping the club when you hit the ball? On a scale of one to ten, with one being very light and ten being very tight, what number would you assign to your grip?

When I ask this question in a group, there are usually a few people who claim a 9 or 10. More will raise their hands when I say the numbers 7 or 8. Some will take the safe road and say 5 or 6. Rarely do I have anyone say they were holding the club at a 3 or a 4, which is, of course where the pressure should be. "THE GOLF CLUB SHOULD BE HELD LIGHTLY, NOT TIGHTLY".

Let me help you own this principle. Make a fist. Squeeze it very tightly; come on and really squeeze it, squeeze, squeeze, a little more, okay, relax. When you relaxed, did you feel the tightness that had occurred in your fingers, wrist, lower arm, upper arm, shoulder, and all the way through to your back? If you need to swing the club freely with your arms and shoulders, and you do, this tightness simply will not allow this freedom of movement to happen.

I know it is only natural to want to grip the club tightly if you want to hit the ball hard, but it simply will not work. Proving once again, **GOLF IS NOT A NATURAL GAME.**

**A** long backswing, with the hands way over the shoulders and the golf club parallel to the ground or even beyond parallel to the ground, is a natural golf swing. Beginners usually feels he or she must hit the ball hard, and in order to hit the ball hard, they feel they must take a long or huge backswing. However, as they start to swing the club forward they realize they don't have a lot of control over the club and therefore they may miss the ball completely. To prevent this they try to slow the swing down as it reaches the ball. This action results in a short follow-through.

Beginning golfers believe they have more control over the club head by slowing the forward swing down when, in fact, they actually lose control over the club because once something is in motion, hitting the brakes will cause an uncontrollable jerking or shaking action. Rather than gaining control, they lose it. If you watch the recreational golfers on the course, you will see a lot of huge backswing and short follow-through swings. Their huge scores also reflect their huge back-swings.

A controlled stroke, that will produce a solid hit, will certainly supply better results than a full swing where you may or may not contact the ball solidly. It may be the natural thing to do to take a full backswing, but it certainly isn't the right thing to do. The follow-through must always be equal to (but can be longer than) the backswing; therefore, you only want to use enough backswing to get the job done.

## A GOLF SWING IS NOT A CIRCLE, BUT A LOW TIRE

It is natural to think of the golf swing as a circle - but it isn't. The swing is actually flat at the bottom. Beginners mistakenly believe that the correct place to hit the ball is where the ball meets the ground as the swing makes a circular motion. If this were the case, you would need to strike the ball perfectly every shot just to get it in the air, and even the pros can't do that. No, the golf ball will fly into the air if it is struck anywhere below its equator; therefore, in order to insure a forward action rather than an upward action, the club head actually stays on the ground a fraction of an inch after it strikes the ball.

### THE MOST IMPORTANT QUARTER INCH IN THE GAME OF GOLF FOR GOLFERS WHO START AFTER THE AGE OF 30

As we move on we will talk about keeping the club head on the "hitting area". The "hitting area" is the beginning of the "target line". The "target line" is a line that looks directly at the target with the ball sitting at the back of the line. It is not enough to strike the back of the ball. It is necessary to keep the club head on the ground for a fraction of an inch (at least a quarter of an inch) after the ball has been struck. The club head actually chases the ball for this fraction of an inch. As soon as the club head starts its upward climb during the follow-through, it will start to veer off the target line. Therefore, it is necessary to keep the club head on the ground for at least a quarter of an inch or more after it has struck the ball. The golf swing actually looks more like a low, car tire than a circle; and if you are not digging up a little dirt AFTER you have struck the ball, you are swinging the club naturally and wrong.

**STOP! Please reread the above**. It is this one action that separates the beginners and hackers from the solid respectable golfers. Respectable golfers drive through, hit through, or sweep through the ball with no thought of getting the ball airborne while beginners and hackers are more concerned about getting the ball to go skyward than they are about getting the ball to go forward.

The club head of a forward golf swing can either be traveling downward, be at the bottom of the swing, or be climbing upward on the follow-through. Because golf is not a natural game, we actually want to catch the ball on the downward swing and have the flat spot or bottom of the swing start at the target side of the golf ball and continue for a quarter of an inch before it starts its climb skyward. This is why any turf you take (a divot) with the club face will be on the target side of the ball after the ball has been struck. In effect, you hit down on the ball to get it to go up. Do you need any more proof that "Golf is not a Natural Game"?

## VISUALIZATION

At the beginning of this section you were asked to imagine you were swinging a golf club. I hope you took the time to imagine these swings in your mind because if you did, you gained a great deal from it. If you didn't, you were playing catch up. Imagination and visualization are MAJOR keys in *Instant Golf.*

A few years ago a research group asked a group of students to shoot some free throws and recorded their scores. The group was then divided into three sub groups. One subgroup was asked to practice fifteen minutes a day shooting free throws, the second group was told not to practice at all, and the third group was asked to only practice shooting free throws in their minds they never missed in their minds. After two weeks, the same students were re-tested. The group who did not practice at all saw no improvement, as expected, and the group who did practice did see improvement, but the surprise came when the group who only practiced in their minds through visualization improved almost as much as the group who actually practiced.

It is this same visualization that allowed a prisoner of war veteran to return to the States and shoot a round of golf in the 70's without having touched a set of clubs for over five years. He claimed he played at least one round of golf in his head everyday he was in the prison camp. Therefore, playing an actual round and scoring well was no big deal. He always played excellent golf in his head. By the way, he had never before scored in the 70's.

Visualization and imagination are powerful tools, and *Instant Golf* cannot succeed without them. When you are asked to visualize or imagine the exercises that follow, please take the time to do so. There once was an oil filter commercial which had a mechanic holding up a filter and saying, "Pay me now (a little bit for a filter) or pay me later" (meaning a major engine repair bill). With *Instant Golf* you can either practice in your mind or at the range. At the range, it is costly and time-consuming. In your mind, it is free and can be done at your convenience; however, one or the other must be done.

## SUMMARY

**T**rying to help or lift the ball into the air, gripping the club with a death grip, taking a huge backswing, or swinging the woods faster or harder than the irons in order to get the ball to go farther are all natural acts that are wrong in the game of golf. *INSTANT GOLF* is designed to help you overcome these natural tendencies in a hurry so you can play SOLID, RESPECTABLE GOLF almost INSTANTLY.

**25**

If you can accept the fact that Golf is not a Natural Game and therefore are committed to learning to do things other than the natural way, you have located the first stepping stone and are ready to locate the remaining three stones that will help you cross over to the island of "Respectable Golfers".

# STEPPING STONE NUMBER TWO

## A SENSE OF TOUCH AND FEEL     (PUTTING)

**Y**our first shot on the golf course is off the tee and the last shot on each hole is usually the putt, so why are we starting with the putt? When you first started to read or write, did you start out with small words or big words? Small words. So it should be in golf. You should start out with the small swing rather than the large one. If you don't buy this explanation, here are a few other reasons to start with the putting stroke.

- The putting stroke is going to be the foundation for over half the strokes you will use on the course.

- Since a putt doesn't leave the ground you can get the feel of hitting the ball solidly without the added pressure of getting the ball airborne.

- Most of us have putted a ball at one time or another. By taking advantage of this fact, we are moving from the familiar to the unknown rather than starting out with the unknown.

**27**

- Putting is where the scoring is. Forty percent of your strokes will be on the putting surface. If you shoot 100, 40 of those strokes may be putts. If you could cut the number of putts down to 30, not an impossible task, you would automatically lower your score to a very respectable 90.

- A missed three foot putt counts as much as a poorly struck ball out on the fairway or off the tee. Since putting does not require a great deal of strength, it is a great equalizer between the big and strong and those who are not quite as big and strong.

- Golf is not rocket science; it is simply a game of putting, chipping and hitting the ball with a full swing. These steps should be learned in this order. Unfortunately too many would-be golfers start out trying to see how far they can hit the ball, and the short game of putting and chipping (over 60% of the strokes in golf) is completely ignored.

- Finally, you can practice putting in your home or office for very short periods of time (10 minutes or less) to develop feel or touch without traveling to a course.

You cannot play any sport that require you to manipulate a ball, i.e., basketball, baseball, tennis, pool etc., without some sense of "feel or touch". It almost brings tears to my eyes to watch a golfer hit a golf ball a country mile and then have no sense of touch or feel around the green. If he or she would just spend ten minutes doing the following exercises, he or she might have some awareness of how to get the ball to roll close to or even into the cup.

**SEESAW TICK-TOCK PENDULUM SWING.**

I gave 100 people putters and balls and asked them to putt the balls to a hole 10 feet away. None of these people had a golf lesson; most did not play golf, and not one of them played golf well. Every one of the 100 did the natural thing of manipulating the putter by snapping or flicking their wrist with a long backswing and short follow-through. Natural but wrong again! As you are about to learn, the putting stroke is almost completely void of any wrist action, that is, if you wish to be a good putter in a hurry. In the old days a number of great golfers were wrist putters, but this action requires a great deal of practice. The putting stroke you are about to learn is done solely with the arms and shoulders and requires no wrist action whatsoever on short putts and very little wrist action on the longer putts. The putting strokes must also be of equal length on each side of the ball.

## Mini Step One

Without a club, go to a nearby wall and stand only far enough away from the wall so you may bend forward. When you do your head should rest against the wall. Fold your arms in front of your chest. Your feet should be placed fairly wide apart, bend slightly at the hips, and using only your shoulders, begin slowly rocking your folded arms back and forth. No leg action or movement, and no head action or movement; just a steady rocking of the shoulders and folded arms as if you were rocking a baby. Notice the shoulders rise and fall like a seesaw, up and down, the folded arms go back and forth.

**D**rop your arms and let them fall towards the floor. Put your fingers and thumbs against one another and point them towards the floor and continue the seesaw action of the shoulders. Notice, as the shoulders go up and down, the arms go STRAIGHT back and STRAIGHT through (like the pendulum of a grandfather clock) along a straight line that could well be a "Target Line." As you swing the arms back and forth, hear the clock going tick-tock, tick-tock, tick-tock. The tick-tock, tick-tock should be steady and smooth.

Some people will have a quick tick-tock while others may have a slow tick-tock. Tall people usually have a slower tick-tock while shorter people do things rather quickly and thus will usually have a quicker tick-tock motion. Once you have established your own tick-tock rhythm or motion, it should never change regardless of the distance you want the ball to travel. The length of the swing will change, but the tick-tock rhythm must remain constant.

**T**he head and the rest of the body must be kept perfectly still. To really get the feel for this action, take a golf club; place it across your chest, and lock it in place by placing the ends under your arms at the arm pits. With your arms hanging down and your fingers together pointing towards the floor, as before, slowly rock your shoulders as you look down towards the floor. Notice the club shaft going up and down, like a seesaw, while your arms go straight back and forth. Also notice the feeling on a perfectly still head. You now have a putting stroke that will allow you to roll the ball towards a target with consistency and without a great deal of effort or practice.

**Why the head must remain still!**

Actually, it is the eyes that we wish to remain still. The eyes are the windows to the brain; and while our brain is a great computer, it can be easily fooled when it comes to motion. Anyone who has ever had his or her car washed at one of those automatic car washes where the brushes rotate around the car can attest to this. The car is in park, with the key turned off; and, if you are like my wife, even the emergency brake is on. But when those brushes pass by your side window, you will still get the feeling the car is moving forward and giving you the urge to step on the brake and stop a car you know is not moving.

If you move your eyes during the putting stroke the mind can not determine if the body moved or the ball actually moved. Since the mind acts automatically in situations where it feels quick action is needed, it will automatically take steps to adjust the swing so you can hit what the brain mistakenly thinks is a moving ball, which of course, is still stationary on the green. This faulty adjustment in the putting stroke will result in a missed putt. Therefore, it isn't head down but eyes down, chin up, and HEAD STILL when putting.

By practicing your putting stroke with your head against the wall, you will develop the feeling of a still head rather quickly. When you have rested your head against the wall, let your shoulders rock up and down like a seesaw with your arms hanging down with your fingers together pointing towards the floor you have completed your first mini step.

It is extremely important you understand the action of the shoulders because this seesaw action is the foundation of the other shots in golf: the "bump and run" and the "simple swing".

**Mini Step Two**

Try the same wall exercise using the putter but without the club shaft across the chest. This time let the outside of the putter head's toe rest against the baseboard of the wall.

**Grip**: The key to a successful putting stroke is placing your hands softly on the club and keeping the wrists inactive for short putts and only slightly active on lag putts. The back of the left hand and the palm of the right hand should face the target. A baseball or softball grip will do as long as the palm of the back hand (for a right-handed golfer the right hand) is facing the target. The putter should be gripped lightly, not tightly (just firm enough that the putter face will not twist in your hands when it meets the ball).

To get the feeling of keeping the wrists out of the

actions, I want you to place a comb, six inch ruler, or pen or pencil under your watch band on the outside of your left wrist and run it down towards your fingers. This should act like a splint and make it impossible or uncomfortable to bend your forward wrist while putting. Your wrist must be locked - inactive. Think of the wrists as being broken and set in a medical cast. Remember, it is natural to want to flick the wrists but - NATURAL IS WRONG.

**B**ack to the wall. Reset your head against the wall, and place the outside of the toe of the putter head against the baseboard. If you prefer, it is okay to bend the elbows a little, providing they do not change position during the stroke. As you perform the up and down movement of your shoulders and your arms start moving like the pendulum of a clock, the baseboard will not only act as a guide for a straight back and straight through stroke, but will also keep the putter's head square (facing the target).

**Mini Step Three**

**F**or this next step you will need a smooth, flat carpet in either your home or office, a putter, a golf ball or two and a dime or some other small flat object to act as a hole.

Place the dime on the carpet in the center of the room. Place the ball two feet away from the dime. Before you start to roll the ball over the dime from two feet away, ask yourself this question: How much power do I really need to nudge the ball to roll three-and-a-half feet or less? Two feet to the dime and no more than 18 inches past the dime. Not very much! Therefore, the follow-through should be very short, and this means the back stroke should also be short. You only want to use enough backswing to get the job done; and, of course, the backswing must be the same length or shorter (never longer) than the follow-through.

## Ball Position

The ball should be positioned directly under the eye that is closest to the target. For right-handed golfers this would be your left eye.

## TOUCH

You are about to have your first lesson in developing touch. Look at the dime and begin to take practice swings, swinging the putter back-and-forth while saying to yourself tick-tock, tick-tock as the putter goes back and forth. The stroke must be of equal length on each side of the ball. It will become very clear, if you have a long forward stroke, you will hit the ball way past the dime two feet away. Don't take my word for it, try it! Try putting the ball with a long, forward stroke and see how far the ball will roll. It is the length of the forward stroke that must be determined first because the length of the forward stroke will determine the length of the back stroke. Again, this is not a natural act.

Since the backswing is the first move in the swing, it is natural to think of its length first. Natural, but wrong. Since you only need a short forward stroke, you must also use a short backward stroke in order to ensure the strokes will be of equal length on each side of the ball.

The equal length of the stroke on each side of the ball is necessary in order to prevent the club head from slowing down at impact. If the club head slows down at impact, you will lose control of the stroke and probably miss the shot. After all, isn't this what happens when we get something heavy like a car going at a high rate of speed and then slam on the breaks? Before anti-lock brakes, did the car stop smoothly or shake a little? It shook a little. So it is with the putter or any other golf club. If you try to slow it down once you have it in motion, it will shake a little and will not hit the ball smoothly or squarely, and the ball will not go where you were aiming.

Stated another way, the back stroke is 1/3 of the stroke and the forward swing is 2/3 of the stroke. 1/3 back and away from the ball. 1/3 back to the ball on the forward stroke and 1/3 past the ball once the ball has been hit. This principle will hold true for any golf swing, around the green, regardless of the club your hold in your hands. Too many golfers give away too many strokes on and around the green because they simply don't understand this principle.

You will not fall into this trap because you know **GOLF IS NOT A NATURAL GAME** and because the 1/3 back and 2/3 through won't let you. What it will do, however, is to force you to focus on how much of a forward swing you will need to get the ball to the hole and then make your backswing correspond with the forward stroke. Only use enough backswing to get the job done.

**35**

There is an invisible line that runs from the target (in this case the dime or hole) through to the back of your ball (The "Target Line"). If you can hit the ball and start it rolling on the target line, and if the carpet is flat, the ball should roll directly over the dime. However, it isn't enough to get the ball to roll over the dime; you must also get it to stop no more than a foot and a half past the target (dime).

The key to making more putts is to get more of the putts to and past the hole. Most weekend or average golfers leave 90% of their first putts short of the hole; and thus, they have no chance of making the putt. However, if you hit the ball so hard it will run more than 18 inches past the cup, should you miss, then it might be traveling too fast to fall into the cup. No one expects you to leave every missed putt only 18 inches past the cup, but this is the goal you should shoot for.

**Why use a dime?**
The diameter of a golf hole is 4 1/4 inches. It will hold three golf balls at the bottom of the cup. If you get used to aiming at a dime, by the time you face a real hole, it will look as large as the Grand Canyon; and you will know if you can roll a ball over a dime, surely you can roll a ball into such a larger hole. With this in mind, once you are able to roll the ball over the dime and get it to stop no more than 18 inches past the dime, you will want to move the ball a little farther away from the dime. Move to three feet, then to four feet, and so forth.
Once you get to six feet, you will want to focus on the Magic Inch in the game of golf called the "Hit-

ting Area" by *Instant Golf.* Stand behind the ball and look at the target (dime). Pick out a spot on the carpet just in front of the ball on the way to the target. If the ball and the putter head travel over the spot you picked out on the carpet, and the putter face is square (looking directly at) to the dime, then the ball must roll towards the dime or target. By focusing on this spot, you have cut a long putt down to a very short one.

## BY THE YARD EVERYTHING IS HARD, BUT BY THE INCH, ANYTHING IS A CINCH.

You might not be able to deal with a 20 foot long lag putt, but you certainly can deal with a spot just in front of the ball that is between the ball and the target.

You not only want the ball to travel over the spot in front of the ball, but you also want the putter head to chase the ball over this spot as well. By focusing on the spot and rolling the ball over it, you know you will have the direction correct. Then you can devote all your concentration on judging the correct distance you want the ball to travel.

**FOR THE SHORT GAME** (putting and chipping) **DISTANCE IS MORE IMPORTANT THAN DIREC- TION.** You will hear this more than once: On long putts and on "bump and run" shots, from off the green, distance is far more important than direction!

### How do you control the distance the ball travels?

You will control the distance the ball will travel with the length of the forward swing. Step away from

**37**

the ball and take a few practice strokes while looking at the hole (in this case the dime). Look at the
length of the forward stroke while focusing your eyes
on the target. As you are taking the practice strokes,
keep repeating the same tick-tock, tick-tock in your
head. Then set up to the ball and line up the shot.
Hear the tick-tock in your head and stroke the ball.
Tick back and Tock through, keeping the same
rhythm as the practice stroke. After a few attempts,
you will amaze yourself how close you come to stopping the ball close to or just past the dime. Remember, distance in lag putting is far more important
than direction.

The Length of the forward swing controls the distance. Determine the forward length you will need
to get the ball to and past the target and then take a
backswing of equal length on the other side of the
ball. The speed of the stroke should never change.
Only the length of the swing changes. If the speed of
the rocking of the shoulders is always consistent,
then the putting stroke will always be smooth and
never herkie-jerkie or choppy.

You must keep the wrists out of the action on
putts. This is why I want you to leave the splint
(comb, pen etc.) under your watchband while practicing. In order for this stroke to be simple, there
can be no movement of any kind except that of the
shoulders going up and down. This will cause the
arms to go back and forth. If at any time you feel
head movement slipping into your putting stroke,
go back to the "head against the wall" exercise and
practice there for a few minutes just to re-establish
the feel of a still head.

## Mini Step Four

**W**hile it is important to know if the ball will go straight or break left or right, a good lag putter will focus 90% of his or her effort on getting the distance correct. If they get the direction correct but run the ball 10 feet past the cup they haven't helped their cause a great deal. If they get the distance correct, but miss the putt 3 feet to the left or right, they have gone a long way in getting down in two.

It is very important that you hit the ball past the dime or by the hole (no more than 18 inches) when on the course. There are two reasons this is important: First, if you get the ball to the hole, it may drop in the hole. There is no chance of this happening if your lag putts are always short of the hole. Secondly, if you do miss the putt and the ball goes past the hole, you can watch it and see which way the ball will break for your next shot. If the ball never gets to the hole, you will be guessing concerning the break on your next putt. In short, you have better odds two ways if you roll the ball with enough power to get it past the hole.

As you get farther and farther from the hole (dime), you may want to get your wrists into the action in order to provide a little power. This action is okay if it is not overly done. Remember, the wrists will be the secondary source of power, not the primary source.

**I** don't suggest you practice putting more than 10 minutes at a time in your home or office, but I do recommend you practice as often as you can or when the mood strikes you. Certainly, you will want to practice putting on a carpet a day or two before you are to go out and play a real game with your friends. "Feel and touch" are so important to the game of golf on or around the green; yet, so many people go to the course without the slightest idea of what it is or how to develop it. *Instant Golf* does not suggest you spend the rest of your life at a practice range; but certainly if golf is worth playing, it is worth spending a little time practicing putting on a carpet in the home or office.

**A**s stated earlier, Putting is where the scoring is. It is also where you will develop that all important sense of "touch or feel." If these are not good enough reasons for you to practice putting in your home or office, how about this one: putting is the shot your playing companions will see you play most besides the tee shots. While on the course they will be too busy with their own shots or too far away from you to notice too much about your shots. However, on the green, everybody will be standing around watching you putt because they want to watch which way your ball will break as it travels towards the hole so they will know which way their ball will break when it is their turn to putt.

If you can play quickly (keep the ball in play) and two putt most greens, then you can play golf with anyone. If you hit the ball well, but it takes you three, four or more putts on every hole to get the ball into the cup, your playing companions will soon tire of your lack of preparation and lose patience with you.

I have had people ask me how practice putting on a carpet can help, especially since the putting greens are grass and not fiber. While it is true the greens will be different from the carpet, it is also true greens on one course will differ from those on another course. The truth is, greens will differ at your local course, even by the hour, as the grass will grow while you are on the course. Rarely will the practice green be the same speed as the greens on the course. The name of the game is adjusting to the conditions at hand. If you have a solid stroke like the Simple See-saw Pendulum Stroke, then adjusting will not be a problem. The idea of practicing on the carpet is to develop confidence in your stroke and to develop some sense of touch without spending a lot of time driving to a course to practice on a real green.

In order to be a decent putter, you will need to learn how and why putts break in one direction or another. Later you will learn when to accept advice from your playing companions and when you must forget it. Having them help you to determine the break of a putt is certainly one of those times when their advice is most welcome.

When you are convinced you have the Simple Seesaw Pendulum stroke down, especially that part about 1/3 back and 2/3 through, you are ready to move to the next step - the "bump and run." How-ever, you are reminded not to leave the Putting Step until you feel very comfortable with it, "A sense of touch" is the second of the four stepping stones you will need to travel to the island of "Respectable Golf-ers." Also, the "bump and run" stroke is built on the same Seesaw, Tick-Tock, Pendulum Swing as the putting stroke.

# STEPPING STONE NUMBER THREE

**MAKE THE BALL GO FORWARD; LET THE CLUB HEAD GET THE BALL INTO THE AIR.**

## AROUND THE GREEN

When your ball misses the green, the first question you should ask yourself is, "Can I putt the ball onto the green and close to the hole?" If the grass is smooth and fairly short and there is no obstacle like sand between your ball and the green, the answer may be yes. Putting from off the green is widely accepted as a wise move. Some even refer to this as the Texas wedge.

**Caution**: For this shot three keys are important:

**1**. A still head and no body movement.

**2**. Focus more on the distance rather than direction.

**3**. Focus on rolling the ball over that magic spot a quarter on an inch in front of the ball and making sure your putter head chases the ball over that spot.

42

**On all shots, especially this one,** you will want to keep hearing the tick-tock, tick-tock in your head as you make the practice strokes looking at the hole and then hearing the same tick-tock as you take the putter back and then through the ball.

**I**f there is too much grass between the ball and the green, your second option is to "bump and run" the ball with your pitching wedge. Others will tell you to use different clubs for the "bump and run", depending on how far away you are from the green or the hole. If you wish to practice a lot, this method works great; but as you will see later, I want you to develop a lot of confidence in a few clubs and know you can make the shot with them rather than trying to play every club in the bag. For our purposes, for the "bump and run" shot, I think you will find it easier if you always use the pitching wedge.

In the section on **GOLF IS NOT A NATURAL GAME** we discussed the natural desire everyone has to want to help or lift the ball into the air. The following story is designed to put this need or natural tendency to bed (in your mind) once and for all. Please pay close attention because when "Hackers" (someone who has been playing golf for awhile and still can't break 100) learn this lesson, they soon see their golf scores fall like the leaves off the trees in autumn.

"**J**enny, Don't lift up. Your job is to get the ball to go forward. It is the clubhead's job to get the ball into the air. If you both do your own jobs, the job will get done."

She attempted to hit the ball several more times. Both times she tried to help or lift the ball into the air. The first effort caught the ground behind the ball as she tried to get the clubface under the ball. The ball did get into the air, but it didn't get very high and did not go very far. Her second effort found the clubface catching the ball near the top of the ball as the clubhead was moving toward the sky in an uppercut fashion. This time the ball rolled along the ground for twenty or thirty yards.

What is going on here? Can't she follow instructions? Does she lack the athletic ability to carry out the instructions? Or, maybe she doesn't believe what she has been told.

(1) She can follow instructions as she has a masters degree in nursing and runs a major wing of a local hospital.

(2) She certainly has the athletic ability because she plays softball and loves to dance.

(3) She may say she understands, but her inner mind is not convinced.

It would be great if we could all learn from others, but the sad truth is, experience is still the best teacher. This student had heard and understood the instructions, but since she had not experienced the results, her inner mind would not buy into it. Only after we have experienced the results, do we really own or buy into the instructions.

**K**nowledge does not equal learning. Knowledge plus belief equals learning, and that belief usually comes from experiencing the event firsthand.

**S**o, how did we help Jenny to own the principle of not trying to help the ball into the air?

We first taught her to putt using the Simple, See-saw, Tick-Tock Pendulum stroke. We then gave her a pitching wedge and told her to putt the ball using the pitching wedge - with the same stroke she used with the putter. Her instructions were to keep the ball rolling on the ground. Surprise, surprise, every time she hit the ball with the pitching wedge, using the putting stroke, the ball jumped into the air. We kept telling her that was not what we wanted. We wanted her to roll the ball ON THE GROUND using the pitching wedge. She couldn't do it! The ball simply would not stay on the ground when struck solidly with the pitching wedge. The only way she could keep the ball from jumping into the air was to hit the ball above its equator.

There is no such thing as a "Hit and Lift" shot in the game of golf. Your job is to move the ball forward; it is the equipment's (golf club's) job to get the ball into the air. The harder you try to help the ball into the air, the more likely it is to stay on or near the ground. The way to get the ball into the air, as Jenny found out, was not to try to get the ball into the air.

Look at the club face of a pitching wedge. While numbers like 48 or 52 degrees do not mean anything to you yet, you can tell the clubface is looking halfway towards the sky as opposed to the putter's face which is looking directly towards the hole along the ground.

The golf club's face is designed to act much like a snowplow's blade. The snowplow's blade throws the snow up in the air and out to one side; yet, the snowplow's blade remains on the surface. Because the pitching wedge's clubface is looking halfway towards the sky, when it strikes the ball, it will throw the ball in that direction (towards the sky) and towards the target.

**W**e will now ask you to try the same exercise we gave Jenny. Take a ball and a pitching wedge and go into your yard or local park. Make sure you are away from people or buildings. Place the ball on the ground and try to putt it a few yards using the pitching wedge. Hit the ball with the pitching wedge just like you would do with the putter. The ball will not roll along the ground. Just like the snowplow, the pitching wedge's clubface will throw what is in front of it into the air without any help from the operator. **PLEASE NOTICE - YOU DO NOT NEED TO LIFT THE CLUBFACE UPWARD OR SKYWARD.** The ball will jump into the air as you keep the clubface low on the ground just as you would do with a putting stroke. If you strike the ball at its back, like you would do if you had a putter in your hand, the ball must go up into the air.

It is natural to think of the golf swing as a perfect circle, but it isn't. If you look at a circle and draw a line for it to sit on, you will see that just a very tiny bit of the circle touches the line. If you believe this is the point you must aim the clubface at in order to der to get the ball airborne, then your margin of error will be very small in deed.

If, however, you think in terms of a low tire rather than a perfect circle, and that the bottom of the golf club should really be on the ground for at least a quarter of an inch or more in order to get that snow-plow-effect, then your margin for error is greatly lengthened.

Hopefully, you have now learned two lessons at once. First, you now own the principle of MOVING THE BALL FORWARD AND LETTING THE GOLF CLUB DO ITS JOB OF GETTING THE BALL INTO THE AIR. Secondly, you have just learned how to play a nice chip shot from just off the green. And now you know why we call it *INSTANT GOLF*.

**BACK TO THE BUMP AND RUN.** (The chip shot)

It is important that this shot be kept low to the ground. You only want the ball in the air just enough to jump over the tall grass or other obstacle between the ball and the smooth putting surface.

With a few minor adjustments, you will execute this shot with the same Simple, Seesaw, Tick-Tock, Pendulum Swing you used for putting. You will want to grip down on the club with your hands closer towards the shaft for better control on the short "bump and run" shots. This will make the pitching wedge shorter and thus accommodate the required shorter stroke.

**B**all Position: Play the ball in the middle of your stance (in front of your belt buckle) for all shots off the green. This will hold true for the shots made

47

from the fairway and off the tee as well.

**H**ead Position: Your head (for all shots off the green) should be behind the ball.

**I**f you have the image in your head of hitting the pitching wedge and seeing the ball jump or hop low into the air and then roll towards the hole from just off the green, you are ready for the Mini Step One of this section.

## Mini Step One

**F**or this step, you need to be in your yard or park with a pitching wedge, a pocket full of golf tees, a shoe box, and a few practice golf balls.

You will want to start on short grass, not heavy or thick grass. If your grass isn't short, then take a few practice swings with the club, which will clip the grass and cut it down to size. One of the problems I see people have with this shot is they keep looking at the grass and don't get the club head down on the ground.

The object of the bump and run shot is to get the ball slightly airborne, and for it to land on or near the green and roll towards the hole.

Place a ball on the ground and place a tee just in front of the ball (almost, but not touching the ball). Which of these objects is the most important? If you said the ball, you are still thinking of golf as a natural game. The tee is the correct answer. If you can get the club head to sweep the tee off the ground, the odds are very good the club head had to travel through the ball and send it towards the target. If you hit the ball but your club head didn't sweep the tee off the ground, the ball may not be heading for the target because it may have been hit with a glancing blow rather than a solid hit. Therefore, we are continuing to stay focused on making sure the club head stays on the ground for a fraction of an inch after it strikes the ball.

Set up in the same stance you used for putting. The ball should be in front of your belt buckle or belly button. Stance is not one of our biggies when it comes to putting or chipping. The goal is to make sure you have a solid foundation and do not have any body movement with the shot. Some people like a wide stance while others prefer a more narrow stance. Some prefer an upright stance while others prefer to bend a little more. For the "bump and run" you just want to be comfortable, and since the legs don't move on this shot, (just like the putt) you want a solid foundation.

Grip down on the pitching wedge for better control for short shots. Take a few practice swings (starting in slow motion and building  up speed) as you  swing  the  club head  of the pitching wedge over the ""hitting area". For the "bump and run" shot you will use the same Simple, Seesaw, Tick-Tock Pendulum Swing as you did for putting. Focus on your shoulders going up and down like the seesaw.

For this step, you are to insert two splint (combs, pens, etc.) into the watchband. One on the outside of your wrist running down towards your fingers as before. The second splint should be on the inside of your wrist running towards the palm of your hand. This should make it almost impossible to bend your left wrist doing the "bump and run" stroke. As you can see, we will go to almost any length to keep you from doing things the natural way - such as flicking or bending your wrist.

Take a few practice swings. As the shoulders move up and down the arms swinging back and forth. The club head of the pitching wedge moves back and forth over the "hitting area" like the pendulum of the clock. Make sure the clubface is looking directly at the target. You are now ready for the next mini step.

## Mini Step Two

Place the shoe box about three feet in front of the "hitting area." Place a ball on a tee. With the ball on the tee, you can focus solely on the stroke rather than on trying to get the ball airborne. Using the Simple, Seesaw, Tick-Tock Pendulum stroke, take a few practice swings looking at the target and hearing the tick-tock, tick-tock of each swing. Set up and take a real swing and strike the ball so it will go into the air, jump over the shoe box, and land just beyond the shoe box. You should still be hearing the tick-tock as you swing while your head should remain down until you hear the ball hit the ground.

What you are developing here is more feel and touch. On a regular green the ball would land on the green and roll maybe ten more feet. In the grass it may just land and stop, but you will have plenty of time to adjust for this on a real course. The idea here is to develop "feel and touch." Remember the NATURAL THINGS TO DO HERE ARE (1) take too long a backswing and (2) try to lift the ball into the air. By now you know if you just strike the ball in the rear with the pitching wedge clubface, the ball will jump into the air. You should also know you only need a "tiny" swing that is equal in length on both sides of the ball to accomplish this feat.

When you feel you are hitting the target 3 feet (one pace), move the target out to 6 feet and then 9 feet. If you are having difficulty hitting the ball a short distance (certainly it is easier to hit the ball farther, like 15 or 20 feet), it may be because you are doing that NATURAL THING of taking a long backswing and using a very short-follow through. Focusing on a 1/3 back and 2/3 through swing will serve you very well.

I want to keep reminding you that you are using the putting stroke here and the putting stroke has no wrist action. We know the natural tendency is to use the wrists the minute we get a club in our hands, but natural is wrong. This stroke is done very simply by rotating the shoulders up and down and this rotation motions causes the arms to go back and forth.

## Mini Step Three

Lower the raised back tee to almost flush to the ground and without a ball take a few practice swings. You will want to focus on keeping the club head low to the ground so place a flat tee just in front of the ball. The ball and the tee will make up the "hitting area." Later you will hit the ball without a tee in front of it, but we will still refer to the ball and flat tee (either real or imaginary) as the "hitting area."

The clubhead should actually brush the ground after it strikes the ball in order to sweep the tee off the ground. If it doesn't, you are not doing the stroke correctly. Place a ball on the flush tee with the tee in front of it and repeat the previous Mini Step starting with hitting the ball only 3 feet over the shoe box. Because the pitching wedge clubface is staying low to the ground like a putt and because you are sweeping the tee off the ground, at no time should you get the feeling you are lifting or trying to lift the ball into the air. Your job, is to get the ball to go towards the target. It is the club's job to get the ball into the air.

Avoid the natural (there is that word again) tendency to look up and see the ball in flight. Keep your eyes on where the ball was until you hear it hit the ground. Then you can look up and follow the roll towards the target. In other words, believe in magic. We talked about the magic "hitting area"; now see the result of that magic by watching the ball disappear from the spot in front of you. Do not look up until you see the ball disappear.

As you try to get the ball to go farther using this stroke you will (1) need to move your hands up on the grip and (2) take a longer backswing and a longer follow-through.

When you get to the practice range, you will want to see how far you can hit the ball using the pitching wedge and the putting stroke. If you rotate your shoulders to the point where your left arm and the shaft of the club are parallel to the ground and with just a little wrist action, you will surprise yourself how far (close to 60 yards or more) you can pitch the ball and yet how deadly your aim can be.

The "pros" in the United States do not use a lot of "bump and run". They prefer to pitch the ball and have it stop near the hole. This is a great shot, but it does require a lot of practice to master. In other parts of the world, especially in Scotland, the "bump and run" is very common. By using the "bump and run" you take a lot of risk out of the shot. You not only have a better chance of getting the distance correct; but by using the putting stroke, you will have a greater chance of getting the ball headed in the right direction.

When you get to the practice range, you will not use the splints, but you should have the feeling they are there in order to keep your wrists inactive. As with the putting stroke, as you get farther away from the hole your wrists will be needed to provide extra power in order to get the ball to travel the required distance. As with the putting stroke, you should resist the use of the wrists as long as possible. When the wrists are needed, make sure they are supplying the secondary source of power, not the main source. Just because the wrists get into the action does not mean the clubface does not remain low to the ground after it hits the ball. You still want to sweep the tee before the clubhead starts its upward climb.

*Instant Golf* does not believe in teaching a lot of different shots as we prefer to have you develop a few shots you have total confidence in and play with those. However, if you need this shot to go to an elevated green and you want the ball to fly high, put the ball more forward in your stance, towards the hole, close to your front foot and continue to use the same putting stroke. This will cause the PW clubface, which might be 50-52 degrees, to become a 56 degree club. Again, use the putting stroke and brush the ground with the clubface once it has struck the ball.

To keep the ball low, play it more in the back of your stance, closer to your back foot.

When you can bump the ball and control the distance (either in your yard or park), you are ready for the Simple Swing.

As stated earlier, anytime you are on the green or around the green, it is wise to look up only after you have seen the ball disappear from its resting spot. For putts shorter than six feet, keep the eyes (head) still until you hear the ball drop into the cup. For longer putts keep the head still until you know the ball has traveled at least six feet. On shots around the green, I advise players not to look up until they hear the ball hit the ground (normally the green). Many a good golf score has been ruined by players' looking up to see how well they hit the shot only to find out their head movement caused them not to hit the shot well at all.

It is not unusual for an average golfer to get within 60 yards of the green in two shots and then spend five or six strokes trying to get the ball into the hole. Hopefully, with this simple stroke, and your head down until you see the ball disappear, you will not suffer this fate.

**Summary**: Just off the green, use the putter if you can. If you can't, use the pitching wedge and the "bump and run." The secret of this shot is to sweep the tee* from in front of the ball with your pitching wedge clubface. You can use this stroke up to 60 yards from the green - if you use just a little wrist action.

*The "Flat Tee" is always placed with the pointed end of the tee pointing towards the would be target.*

# STEPPING STONE NUMBER FOUR

## SHORT AND RELIABLE IS BETTER THAN LONG AND UNRELIABLE!

**Golf is a game of effortless power, not powerful effort.**

THE SIMPLE SWING  (How not to swing like a pro and still play solid, respectable golf)

**Y**ou now have two legs of a three-legged stool. That is to say that 2/3 of the golf strokes can be played with a pitching wedge, a putter and a putting stroke. With few exceptions, anytime you are within 60 yards of the green (give or take 20 yards depending on your strength), you can use the pitching wedge. Nevertheless, a three-legged stool can't work without the third leg. Okay, you do need a golf swing, but do you need the classic pro-type swing?

**B**efore we begin talking about the swing, let me tell you my famous pile driver story.
  Picture yourself walking on a midway of a local fair on a summer afternoon when you hear a voice, "Can you lend me a hand?"  You look and it is a

**56**

church group putting up a huge food tent, and they want you to help them drive a few stakes. Actually, all this guy wants you to do is hold the stakes while he hammers them into the ground.

As you start to hold the stake and see the large pile driver you decide to ask a question, "Have you ever done this before"?

"No, or only a few times" is not the answer you wanted to hear.

Assuming he doesn't do this often, which style would give you the most comfort? Would you prefer him to take the hammer back a short distance and make a controlled swing or is it all right with you if he just takes that big hammer way back over his head and brings it down to the stake with the full force of his body. Now I don't know about you, but if he swings that pile driver like he is trying to ring the bell on the midway game, my hand isn't going to be holding the stake as the pile-driver heads towards it. Why? Too large a chance for error because that huge back swing and long down stroke have too many moving parts, and if any of them are not working together (a good possibility for someone who doesn't do this act very often), the head of the hammer might very easily miss it's mark and crush my hand.

Now, if the head of the hammer is much larger than the head of a golf club, and the head of the stake is much larger than a golf ball, and there is some doubt that these two will meet solidly with a full swing, what chance do you see of the small head of a golf club repeatedly striking a small golf ball solidly with such a large swing?

For those of you who have played a little golf, does this next story sound familiar?

"How did you play?"

"Same old stuff, on 14 holes I had nothing but bogeys (one over par with par being what a very good golfer should do on the hole) and a few pars; but, as usual, I always have those 3 or 4 bad holes where I hit the ball into the water or out of bounds. I tell you those 8's and 9's really kill my score."

Or how about this one.

"How did you play"?

"I don't know what is wrong. I went out to the driving range the other night and hit the ball perfectly. I mean I hit them 250 yards straight as an arrow and then I went out to the course and couldn't get off the tee. I was out-of-bounds or in the woods on three of the first four holes. I was 10 over par before I got to the fifth hole."

**W**hat is wrong is something very simple. These golfers are trying to swing like the pros on TV. The classic pro-type swing has many moving parts (even more than the pile-driver because the pile-driver is only going up and down and the golf swing is not only going up and down, but backwards and forwards). If you thought the pile-driver swing had a lot of moving parts, you can guess how many more moving parts are in the classic pro-type golf swing. If you thought the pile-driver might miss the stake and hit your hand, what do you think the odds are of a golf club striking that small ball solidly when being propelled by a swing with so many moving parts?

Let's see now. On the back swing the pros will tell you how to shift your weight to your back foot as you start the club back with a one piece take-a-way, whatever that is. They will tell you how and where and what your hands should be doing, how and what your hips should be doing, how and what your shoulders should be doing and how and what your legs and feet should be doing, on the back swing. The end result is to get your hands well above your head, the club shaft parallel to the ground and pointing towards the target, your weight on your back leg and foot, your hips turned at a 45 degree angle away from the ball, and the shoulders turned 90 degrees away from the ball as your back is facing the target. Your body is now coiled like a loaded spring. Oh, by the way, don't forget to relax! Darn, I forgot to mention the "swing plane."

If you are supple enough, or if you are a contortionist, you might be able to do this because the back swing is done in slow motion. However, the forward swing is done in a split second, and the pros want your body to do far more complicated things on the way down than it did on the way up.

We have already talked about the problems of starting down before the back swing is completed; however, one of the main concerns of the classic pro-type swing is the double-movement action of the hips. On the down swing the hips are supposed to move forward 4 to 6 inches and then do a sharp left hand turn. The pros call this "clearing out the left side". This move is difficult to learn; and because it is a timing thing, it requires a lot of practice to maintain.

Pros talk about maintaining their body position during the swing, but films of their swings show their bodies actually moving in three directions (downward, backward and forward) at the same time.

They are able to keep this kind of swing together and in sync because they learned it by rote as a youngster and maintain it by practicing almost daily. If you didn't learn it as a child and you can't practice daily, as the pro do, what chance do you possibly have of having a consistent swing with a swing that has this many moving parts? We are back to slim and none.

What is amazing is we can actually do at least some of these gyrations perfectly some of the time. If we couldn't do them at all, we would find another way to accomplish what we want to accomplish, but the golf gods have pulled a cruel joke on golfers who start over 30. They allow them to find a little success with this swing and this leads them to believe if they will just practice long enough, or just spend enough money on lessons, or just concentrate hard enough, they will be able to do this act swing-after-swing. Of course they can't.

While it is true these golfers may get the swing in sync at the range, they can never be assured it will be in sync when they arrive at the course. On the course they may not have the swing in sync during the first three holes and thus already be six or seven over par. Then they find the swing and play decent golf but beat themselves up for not doing better earlier in the round. Of course their playing companions may have a different story. Swing well at first and lose it towards the end of the round and maybe the most common of all experiences is to hit one great shot and then flub the next only to follow the flub with another great shot.

Golfers, who start late in life, keep hoping for that impossible dream. They truly believe they will at least come close to keeping this impossible swing in sync for 18 holes. Heaven help them if for one day they are able to do so; because, when they go back out on the course and don't have it, they will hate themselves and the game even more.

The Simple Swing will not make you a perfect golfer, but it will make you a consistent one. The great golfer Bobby Jones once did an instructional film in which he explained the way he swung a golf club. He wanted to state very clearly his wasn't the only way, nor would he say it was the best way. What he would said was, "It was the way he did it with some degree of success."

**I** am not trying to convince anyone that the Simple Swing is the best swing or that the pros should use it. What I am saying is it is the simplest, easiest, most repeatable, and therefore the most dependable swing to learn in the shortest period of time. It is also far easier on your back than the classic pro-type swing which can play havoc with even the best of adult backs. The Simple Swing is a consistent swing; and most importantly, you will not be penalized for not learning it as a child and thus you won't need to spend hours on the practice range trying to master it.

I don't care if you play golf only once a week or once a year. When you go to the course, the swing will be there and you won't need to deal with those intangibles like timing or getting your swing in sync. Unlike a pro-type swing this swing does not have many moving parts. The shoulders rotate back just like they did on the putting stroke, and the belly button turns away from the "hitting area" and then turns back and then through the "hitting area", and all of this is supported by the back leg (right leg).

Since your hands never get above shoulder height, all those terrible things that can happen at the top of the back swing, like lifting your head or swaying off the ball, re-gripping the club, having the club off plane, starting down too quickly, coming over the top (throwing the club away from your body and to the outside of the target line), and uncocking your wrists too soon are automatically eliminated.

Fewer moving parts means a more-dependable swing. I have a friend who has a 12-cylinder sports car. When it is in tune it runs like a top, but he has a hard time keeping it in tune. When it is out of tune, you don't want to be near the car as it runs and sounds so bad. My neighbor, on the other hand, has an economy car (four-cylinders - fewer moving parts). Not very pretty, not very flashy, but oh so dependable. *Instant Golf* advocates dependability over flashy because dependability will allow you to always enjoy the game while flashy will only allow you to enjoy the game on those occasions where everything works just right.

**W**hen you swing a golf club there are only three result that matters:

1.  The head and body must be behind the "hitting area" as the club head passed through it. This should always be your major concern. It is natural to lung forward when you swing a golf club. If you do not making a concerted effort to keep your head and body behind the ball at impact, it is very easy to fall into the habit of lunging and therefore getting your head and body ahead of the ball before impact. If the head and body get ahead of the ball before the ball is struck, then the ball has no chance of going where you want it to go.

2.  The club head must pass through the "Hitting Area." If you make a circular swing (a natural act), the club head will only catch the ground at one tiny spot; and if that isn't the correct spot, you will not hit the ball solidly or cleanly. Making the club head travel through the hitting area (club head stays on the ground at least a quarter of an inch after impact to sweep the tee) will increase you chances of a solid hit by a large margin.

3. The club face must be looking at the target while passing through the "hitting area." You must do this at all cost even if it means swinging at only 50% of your power. How can a ball go straight if it is struck with a glancing blow?

<u>If you accomplish these feats, nothing else matters; and if you can't accomplish these feats,  nothing else matters.</u>

The ball does not care how you stand or grip the club or anything about how you arrived at accomplishing these three feats. Any way you can do it consistently should be okay with you and your friends.

The key word is consistently, because hitting the ball 250 yards in the fairway only 2 out of 5 times, using a long back swing, with the other three landing in trouble will not get the job done. *Instant Golf* will tell you what your arms, hands, head and belly button should be during the swing, but anyway you can swing the golf club to accomplish these three simple tasks will do.

The fewer moving parts you have in your swing, the easier it will be to get the club head and club face to do what you want them to do. Swinging the club with a big back swing (even if you swing it slowly) and of course doing those other natural things we discussed earlier are acts that will hinder your ability to reach these objectives. By the way, if you aren't going to use a long back swing then there is no reason to have a lot of unnecessary movement with your feet and legs either.

**B**efore we leave this subject, let me make one more point. The first time you pick up a golf club, on a golf course, it is natural to think, "That hole is sure a long way away. I'll really need to hit the ball hard if I ever want it to reach the putting surface." Rarely, does anyone think, "I better focus on hitting the ball straight, otherwise it will go into the woods or weeds." By now you know that distance is more important than direction in the short game (putting and the "bump and run"), but direction is far more important than distance off the tee and up to 60 yards or so from the green.

Don't make the mistake of thinking, as so many pros teach, that you will learn to hit it hard first and learn to straighten it out later. Kids learn this way and it works great for them, but as adult you will never have the time or talent to work on straightening out a long ball later. It is far better as an adult to learn to hit it straight first and work on distance later. At least doing it this way, you will be spending more time in the fairway than in the rough.

**E**nter the Simple, one-legged, belly button swing! If you only had one leg, as one golfer did, you would not be able to slide forward without losing your balance. By simply turning on his back leg he was able to hit the ball as far or farther than most two-legged, amateur golfers. He played to a 2 handicap. His swing proved the sliding action of the hips, which causes so many golfers so much trouble, was an unnecessary move.

Even though the one-legged swing is a simple swing, it is also a powerful swing because it creates a great deal of centrifugal force. Remember when you were a kid and played "crack the whip"? The kids in the center of the human chain barely moved while the kids on the outside of the chain had to run like hell to keep from falling down.

So it is with this golf swing. The turn around your back leg will generate a lot of power from the center of your body to the club head extended away from the center of the body. The club head thus becomes those kids on the outside of the chain.

If you are a beginning golfer, what you are about to learn will be easy for you, however; if you have played golf for awhile (without a great deal of success), what you are about to read will be a lot different from the pro-type swing you have been trying to use. You may have to unlearn a few things like shifting the weight from one side to the other during the swing.

The Simple Swing revolves (that is not a pun, it is a fact) around the back leg (the right leg if you are right handed) of the golfer. The weight is set up on the back foot and leg with the knee slightly bent as if one was sitting on a barstool. The golfer simply turns around his or her back leg by rotating their shoulders and belly button away from the target and then turns their belly button towards the target. The shoulders, arms, and back knee along with the golf club, will follow the belly button. The weight remains on the back foot as long as possible and only shifts to the front foot to prevent you from falling down after the arms and club head have swung through the hitting area.

**Ok, so you turn around your back leg, but how**

**do you hit the ball and make it go where you want it to go?**

Think, **TST. T**urn, **S**weep and **T**oss.
**Turn** on or around your back leg. **Sweep** an imaginary tee that is laying flat on the ground, pointing towards the target and slightly in front of the ball, and feel as if you are **tossing** the club head directly towards the target, should you let the club fly out of your hand.

If you have enough room in your yard or park, and if you have an old golf club (hopefully an iron) and without a ball, you can try this **Turn, Sweep** and **Toss** move and actually throw the club towards the target (away from people and buildings). Try it using only your right hand if you are right-handed, and then try it with both hands on the club. The first couple of tosses may seem a little wild, but, after a few tries, you should begin to get the hang of it.

The flat tee should be placed where a ball would normally be placed (in front of your belt buckle), and the idea here is to sweep it off the ground. If you will turn on your back leg, sweep the tee and imagine you are tossing the club head towards the target, you will have a beautiful, powerful, repeatable golf swing that will allow you to hit the ball in play on or near the fariway
   Forget what is natural, forget anything and everything you have ever read or heard about swing planes, wrist cocks, releases, weight shifts, etc. The golf swing is nothing more than a **TURN, SWEEP AND TURN** motion.

By turning your bellybutton around the back leg you will get all the body rotation you need to hit with power. By sweeping the tee you will be driving through the ball, rather than trying to <u>hit</u> at it or trying to lift it into the air. By having the feeling you are tossing the club towards the target, you will be swinging the club down the target line rather than coming across the line and swinging the club towards left field. The tossing action also provides you with a wrist cock on the backswing and a release when you are sweeping the tee.

## How can you mess up such a simple swing?

As simple as this swing is, it can be messed up if you try hard enough. If you take such a huge backswing that you aren't able to locate the flat tee on the down stroke you will mess up the swing.

Swinging so hard that you end up off balance will mess up the swing. Trying to hit at or hit the ball, rather than sweeping the imaginary tee in front of the ball will cause you to top the ball or hit behind the ball.

I have never seen anyone try to sweep a floor without letting the broom actually touch the floor. Yet, I have had both men and women tell me they are sweeping the tee although their clubhead never touches the ground. You not only want the clubhead to touch the ground you actually want it to stay on the ground for 1/4 to 2 inches after it strikes the ball. Sweeping the imaginary tee will automatically provide you with this motion.

Finally, failure to throw the club in the direction of the target will mess up the swing. If the ball is always going to the left, it is because you are throwing the club head in that direction rather than the direction of the target. When you swing the club up it will want to go left. Your job is not to swing the club skyward but forward as if you are reaching out towards the target. One common fault here is when you reach out with your hand and arms towards the target you will have a tendency to let your head go forward as well. Natural but wrong. <u>You must keep the head behind the ball as you reach and stretch your hands and arms towards the target.</u>

### Turn, Sweep, and Toss. That's it?

That's it! If you are doing anymore than this you are trying to make the game more difficult than it is.

Just as you can practice putting at your home, and just as you can practice chipping in your backyard or park, so you can practice the swing in your yard or park. Simply lay a tee flat on the ground and try to sweep it off the ground. Start in slow motion and gradually build up speed until you are unable to consistently sweep the tee. Now you know you are swinging to fast/hard or your backswing is to long. Actually, usually your backswing is to long, because, I have found you can swing fairly hard and sweep the tee if you have a shot backswing, because you only have a few moving parts: however, if you take a long backswing and try to slow it down, you still have all those moving parts that can get out of sync and therefore the reliabilty you desire is unobtainable.

When you feel comfortable sweeping the tee off

the ground using, say, a pitching wedge, place a plastic practice golf ball (you can buy these at any discount or sporting good store) in front of your belt buckle and place the flat tee about a 1/4 to 1/2 inch in front (to the left of the golf ball if you are right handed) of the ball. Now **swing** and **sweep** the tee without looking at the ball. If you sweep the tee, the ball should simply get in the way of the club head as it travels towards the tee. If this happens you will be striking the ball with a slightly down-ward blow and the ball should jump into the air. Golf is not a natural game.

Don't worry where the plastic ball goes as long as it goes into the air. <u>If it didn't get into the air you did not sweep the tee.</u> Practice this swing with a pitching wedge until you are comfortable not look-ing at the ball but looking at the flat tee. When you are comfortable just sweeping the tee, remove it and just put the plastic ball in front of your belt buckle and imagine the tee being front of the ball. Now sweep the tee that isn't the air. You are now ready for the practice tee.

There is one exercise I do insist you do in your home or office before you go to the practice range. Place a nickle where the ball would normally be on a flat, smooth carpet. Take your stance, grip the club lightly with a baseball (10 finger) grip and place the club face of the pitching wedge directly behind the nickle. Without a back swing, slowly push the nickle along the carpet towards the target. Your head and body must remain still and behind the spot where the nickle was originally. When you reach the point where you must either move the body forward to keep the club head on the carpet or let the club head leave the carpet **STOP** and **freeze the action**. You will notice the right arm is straight and you get the feeling your right arm and club shaft are reaching for the target. This is the feeling you want to feel just after you have struck the ball. At no time do you want to feel you are swinging the golf club skyward before you have reached this "sweeping, reaching feeling".

# PRACTICING AT THE RANGE
## Sweep the Flat Tee - pointing toward the target

When you go to the practice range, take 50 or more tees with you. When you sweep the tees off the mat you may not be able to recover them. This is okay, because the lesson will cost you some money; therefore, it will be a hard lesson to forget. Find a mat and place a flat tee on in. Take a pitching wedge and grip it lightly with the 10 finger baseball grip and allow your right thumb pad to cover your left thumb which should point down the shaft. If you prefer, you can let your little finger of the lower (right) hand to overlap the index finger of the upper hand. Put all your weight on your back foot and cross your front (left) foot behind your right with little or no weight on it. The flat tee should be just in front of your belt buckle.

In slow-motion swing the pitching wedge back by rotating your shoulders just like you did doing the putting stroke. However, this time you want to extend the stroke as if you were trying to hand the club head to someone standing about five feet to the right of you. As you extend your left arm in that direction, the belly button will turn away from the hitting area. For this exercise do not take the club above shoulder height and do not break or cock your wrists.

Still in slow-motion turn your belly button back

to the hitting area and let your shoulders, arms, and hands follow. Strike the flat tee and sweep it from the mat. Continue turning on your legs (together) to a follow-through where your right arm is reaching out in the direction of the target and then swinging upward rather than swinging towards the sky as soon as the tee is hit. Reset the tee. Do the swing over and over again gradually building up speed until you are swinging so fast that you are unable to sweep the tee away.

Yes, you must strike the carpet on this swing; and if you don't allow the club head to stay on the carpet through the "hitting area," you simply will not be able to sweep the tee.

**This practice exercise is designed:**

**1**. To get you to develop the feeling of rotating around the back leg.

**2.** To develop the feeling of staying behind the ball because if you move your upper body forward on the forward swing you will lose your balance, and end up pulling the ball rather than hitting it with power.

**3**. To develop the feeling of letting the club face acts like a snowplow and sweep the tee off the carpet. You can't move on to the next exercise until you are confident you can sweep the tee off the carpet swing-after-swing.

**4.** To emulate a motion of tossing the clubhead towards the target.

To help you develop the sweeping action try this exercise: Take the same stance as before. Bend over as if you were going to address the ball. Hold the pitching wedge in your left hand and place the club head on the ground in front of your left breast pocket. Hold the shaft straight up and down with your left arm out straight and parallel to the ground. Keep your head still and throw your right hand and arm under your out stretched left arm.

This should give you the feeling of staying down on the swing and throwing your right hand and arm at the target rather than lifting the right arm towards the sky. When you swing the golf club and sweep the tee you should have the same feeling of reaching for the target with your right hand and arm rather than reaching for the sky on the follow-through.

## The Set Up or Stance and building a swing

Believe me, the Set-Up is more important than the swing itself because, without a solid foundation, your golf swing will be built on sand.

Set up to the ball with the ball in front of your belt buckle or belly button and place a flat tee just in front of the ball. The tee should almost touch the ball. Spread your feet about the width of the inside of your shoulders. Point the toes out slightly in a duck-like fashion. For the time being, your knees should be locked as you are standing as tall as you can.

Look at your forward (left if you are right handed)

foot. Notice the spot where the heel is sitting. Lift up your forward foot. When you do you will have 100% of your weight on your back foot. Set your forward foot back down by placing the sole of your shoe where your left heel was originally. You can then let your heel also return to the ground but keep 75% to 80% of your weight on the heel of your back (right) foot. This is referred to as an "open" stance since your hips are now "open" to the target.

Bend slightly from the waist (the pros bend from the hips). You want your right shoulder to be directly above the shoelaces of your right shoe. If your shoulder is beyond your toes, you have bent over too far.

With the outside of your right index finger tap the ligament behind your right knee cap. This will cause your right leg to bend slightly. It is also a signal for your left knee to relax and bend slightly, but not as much as the right knee. This move will also cause your right shoulder to dip and your left shoulder to rise. This will also cause your head to move to the right and behind the ball. Leave it there. You should now have the feeling you are sitting on a bar stool with your back foot on the floor and with little or no weight on the front foot. You are not bending way over, but are sitting on the back leg and foot.

I repeat, please make sure that 75 to 80% of your weight is sitting on your back (right) heel. You have heard the expression "Swinging from his heels"? In baseball it is a home-run swing; and while we use this swing because it is simple and easy to learn, we also want it to be a powerful swing as well.

Place a golf glove or other soft object under your

left armpit and hold it in place by resting your upper left arm against your left chest. Do not let the glove fall out at anytime during the swing.

Address the ball by placing the club head behind the ball and forming a straight line from your left shoulder, left arm and club shaft. It was okay to bend the arms a little in the putting and chipping strokes; but for this swing you need the forward (left if you are right handed) arm to be in a straight line with the shoulder, club shaft and the ball.

Keeping most of your weight on your back foot (actually on the heel), once again slowly turn your belly button and rotate your shoulders away from the "hitting area". As you do, stretch out your left arm as if you were trying to put the club head into the hands of someone standing five feet to the right of you. Do not, however, let the glove fall from your left armpit. Let the left arm take the club slightly beyond parallel to the ground, and you will want to let your wrists bend just a little at the top of the swing.

If you have played golf before, this wrist cock is 1/4 the size of a normal wrist cock. If it were any less, there wouldn't be a wrist cock. At no time should you bend the wrists so much that the shaft of the golf club is pointing straight up towards the sky as if you are holding an umbrella. At this point your left knee should have bent a little and should be facing the hitting area (you might let your left foot roll a little to the right, but it is not recommended that you allow the left heal to lift off the ground during the back swing). At the top (which is actually the middle of most golfer's back swing) your belly button should be pointing towards the toes of your right foot.

You are now ready to start the down or forward swing: Start the forward move by simply turning your belly button back to the ball and then towards the target.

Your arms, left knee, and hip will automatically rotate to the left and your right shoulder and the right knee will follow the belly button. Your body will turn on the right leg with the knee moving forward, and your head will remain still and behind the "hitting area" as the club head drives through the "hitting area" (driving through the "hitting area" means striking the ball before the turf and then sweeping the tee from the mat (or turf) after the ball has been struck). Your right arm will reach out towards the target and then climb skyward. At some point your weight will need to be transferred to your forward foot in order to prevent a loss of balance. This is okay. We simply want the weight to follow the swing, not lead it. At no point during the swing should you drop the glove under your forward armpit.

Just like you did when your feet were together, start the swing in super slow-motion, and then reset the ball and tee and repeat the swing over and over, gradually building up speed until you are unable to keep your balance or unable to sweep the tee off the mat. When this occurs, you are swinging too fast and you need to back the swing down to a speed you can handle.

Remember your number one priority: hitting the

ball solidly and keeping the head and body behind the ball while doing so. Swinging so fast or hard that you are unable to accomplish these acts will defeat your entire effort. You must accomplish these feats even if you must swing at only 50% of your full power. However, with a short back swing you will find that you will in time be able to consistently strike the ball solidly with 80-90% of your maximum power. The long back swing golfers, who didn't learn as youngsters, will never be able to make that statement.

**NOTE**. Some people have no idea of how far they are taking the club back on their back swing. They believe they are only taking a half swing when in fact the club is behind their head and shoulders. At the top of your back swing stop or freeze the action. Turn your head directly to the right of you. If you can't see both hands you have gone back to far.

Also, check the thumbs. They should be pointing away from the target, not towards the sky or the target.

The faster you turn your belly button towards the "hitting area," the faster the club head will be traveling when it passes through the "hitting area". The faster the club head is traveling when it strikes the "hitting area," the farther the ball will travel providing it is struck solidly. You should see how fast you can turn your belly button and swing the club. When you get to the point you can no longer control the club and make it perform those two other critical acts of looking at the target and traveling down the "target line" through the "hitting area," then you know you have gone too far and you will need to back the swing down just a little. Remember the first critical point is to keep the head and body behind the ball.

For those of you who have played golf before I hope you will realize you can swing the golf club faster and thus drive the ball farther because you have total confidence you will strike the ball solidly and it will then go where you want it to go.

Do not try to manipulate the club face on the back swing. The pro-type swing tells you to get the toe of the club face pointing towards the sky on the way back, and it should be pointing towards the ground once the club shaft is over your shoulders and behind your neck. This is just another moving part that can get out of sync and is simply not needed. In the Simple Swing the club face of any club acts like the club face of a putter. It simply goes away from the ball and then goes back and through the ball.

The "simple swing" uses an abbreviated back swing. The hands should never get above the right shoulder and the wrists should never get fully "cocked" like the pros suggest. The question is asked, "why do we do it this way"? We do it this way because the full swing and the wrist cock are both highly overrated and are the main reasons all those moving parts can't work together.

John Cook, the former U.S. Amateur Championship, 1993 Ryder Cup member, and a PGA tour professional, who has finished in the top 50 on the "money list" for five years in a row, uses a similar abbreviated back swing with great results.

Robert Landers, used a comparable swing to qualify for the Sr. PGA Tour even though he had never had a professional golf lesson and played golf in sneakers.

Or take the case of Ralph Markin of Urbana, Ohio. The other day he shot a 34 (2 under par) on the back nine of his local course. He normally plays that nine, 2 over par.

What makes this noteworthy? Ralph is 79 years old and didn't take up the game until he was 57. When I heard the story, I visited with Ralph. I was afraid he might have been the exception to the rule and actually did learn to swing like a pro after the age of 30. "Not so", according to Ralph. "He never had a lesson."

"When did you really start to get good at the game?" I asked.

He told me, when he was 59, he had developed a very good short game, but couldn't keep his drives in the fairway. One day a playing companion told him his back swing was to long. Ralph tried a shorter, more compact back swing and found out his "banana" ball became a straight ball and his scores began to fall like Newton's apples. I guess had he wanted to, he could have written this book twenty years ago.

A short back swing and long follow-through is far more valuable than a long back swing and a short follow-through. Many adult women are very supple and are able to get their hands and arms well above their heads; but if they slow the golf club down on the downstroke, because they fear missing the ball if they don't, they have not helped themselves at all. Rather than slowing down, we want the club head to gain speed as it approaches the hitting area. Slowing down the club head once it is in motion towards the hitting area, is a sure way to lose control of the swing. What you want is to take a comfortable back swing and turn quickly and powerfully into the "hitting area" with your belly button and shoulders.

You will notice that I keep referring to the "hitting area". It is to your advantage to think of the ball and the flat tee as the "hitting area" because you want to drive the club head through the ball and sweep the tee from the ground. If you think of only hitting the ball, you may strike at only the ball rather than swinging through the ball.

When you are confident, you can strike the ball solidly and sweep the tee off the mat using the pitching wedge, move down to the eight iron and start the process all over again. Continue this exercise with the six iron and the seven or five wood or both.

The key to this swing-exercise is sweeping the tee and doing it in slow-motion and building up to a comfortable speed. Remember the slogan: Short and Reliable is better than long and unreliable.

It is extremely difficult to hit the ball and sweep the tee swing-after-swing with a long back swing. The higher your hands go above your shoulders and the more wrist cock you have in your swing (moving parts), the more inconsistent and unreliable your swing will become.

Sure, at the beginning your best shot with a long back swing will be better than your best shot with a short back swing; however, over time this will not be true. More importantly, your poor shots with the long back swing will be far worse than your poor shots with a short back swing. The long back swing is flashy and will lead to lots of peaks and valleys in your golf game while the short back swing will lead to a consistent game swing-after-swing.

You are now ready for the turf. Before you move off the mats, remember the key points. Your objective is to strike the ball and sweep the tee while the club face is looking at the target. An abbreviated back swing will help you repeat this move swing after swing. How you grip the club or how you take your stance is no one's business but your own.

I can assure you a long, classic, pro-type swing is not a repeatable swing for anyone taking up the game after 30. As mentioned earlier, as long as you stay behind the ball upon impact and can sweep the imaginary tee from in front of the ball, any controlled swing will do: the shorter it is, the easier it is to do consistently.

I once taught a dentist the Simple Swing with the abbreviated back swing. After a few minute he was hitting the ball 220 yards straight over the 200 yard sign at the driving range. Later I saw him on the course, and he was back to his huge back swing with all its moving parts. When I ask him why he returned to his huge swing he told me, "I get a bigger thrill out of crushing the ball than I do out of hitting it straight all the time. I know you told me I will never be consistent with a huge swing, and my logical side believes you, but deep-down in my gut, I just keep thinking, if I can hit it 250 yards down the middle once, I should be able to do it all the time, and of course I want to do it all the time."

There are lots of things we would all like to do, but simply aren't capable of doing. This dentist is not big enough, or fast enough, or young enough, to become a pro football or basketball player, and <u>he isn't going to become a consistent golfer using his long classic pro-type swing either!</u>

Life is always about options. The dentist had two options: 1) Play solid, respectable golf, or 2) be macho man and swing like the pros. He chose macho man. We should all play golf for the enjoyment of the game and if this is the way he enjoyed playing the game; then this is the way he should play the game; but it won't be as much fun for his playing companions as they will need to continue to listen to him complain when one of his shots goes astray and, to add insult to injury, they will need to pretend they are enjoying themselves while they search for his lost balls.

Some golfers, who couldn't bring themselves to give up their long back swing altogether, have agreed to cut their back swings down while using the irons, but insist on using a long back swing off the tee and for fairway woods. I guess a half-a-loaf is better than no-loaf and hopefully these golfers will soon realize they are more consistent with their irons than their woods and will start swinging the woods with the same abbreviated swing they use with the irons.

## CAUTION

One final word before you move to hitting the ball off the turf.

<u>Do not move to the turf from the mat until you are sure you are actually sweeping the tee rather than trying to "pick" the ball off the mat</u>. You must let the "snowplow" work. The club head, once it has hit the ball must stay on the ground and target line for a fraction of an inch before it starts moving skyward.

This point is so important that I can't over emphasis it enough. It is natural to want to "lift" or "pick" the ball off the ground - but it is wrong! You must allow your club face to hit the ground after you have hit the ball.

NOT THIS
a circle

BUT THIS
a low tire

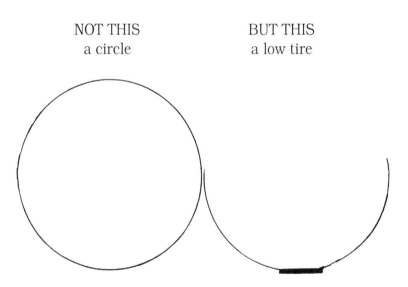

This and the one before it are the only illustrations in the book, so they must be important!

In this illustration the ball has been struck and the club head and the right arm are reaching forward towards the target. The club head has swept the tee from in front of the ball.

NOTICE, there is no lifting action of any kind in this swing. You must resist the natural temptation to swing the club skyward too early. Also notice the head is still and behind the "hitting area".

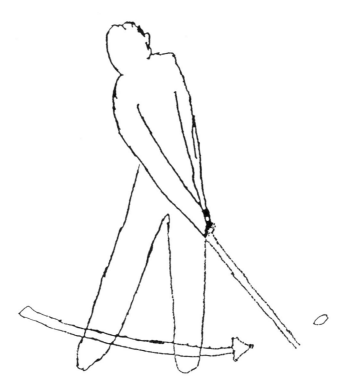

# HITTING OFF THE TURF

You must select a range that allows you to hit from the turf. Hitting off a mat is okay for the flat tee-drill, but not for learning to actually hit the ball.

Take your pitching wedge, 8 iron, 6 iron, 7 wood (if you have one, and if you don't I suggest it is money well spent to get one), and 5 wood out to the turf with a large bucket of balls.

As you are walking to the area, where you can hit off the grass, notice some of the other golfers hitting golf balls. Don't focus on the golfers who seem to be knocking their balls out of sight and straight, but select a few who don't seem to be doing very well. These are the ones who are not making solid contact with the ball or whose balls seem to be flying off in all directions. Notice how many people at the range fit this description (at least half), and these are the golfers who are practicing and trying to improve.

Can you detect them violating any of the things you learned about golf not being a natural game or about the problems caused by a full back swing? You are watching to see if you can spot some of the problems as well as building your own confidence as in, "hey, I think I can already do better than that."

When you get on the course, there will be plenty of golfers just like these. There will also be many more who haven't bothered to practice but will nevertheless be trying to swing like a pro. By now I hope your confidence is building and some of your nervousness is going away.

## SQUARE BREATHING

Nervousness on or around the driving range as well as on the course seems to be something all beginners share. When we get nervous, we can't think clearly. Some students, who always study, can't seem to make good grades. They get nervous and simply do not take tests well. Square Breathing can help them, and it can help you at the range and on the course. To relieve tension or nervousness we need to get oxygen into our lungs and then to our muscles, especially our brain. Just taking deep breaths won't get it done, so try this.

Take a deep breath and count to four while doing so. Hold your breath for four counts and then exhale and count four beats while doing so. Count four more beats before you take your next breath and then start the whole process all over again. It sounds simple; but I can assure you, after a few complete cycles, your tension or nervousness will be greatly reduced, and you will be able to recall the things you have learned from this course.

## THE PRE-SHOT ROUTINE

Prior to setting up to hit the ball, you will want to go through a pre-shot routine. A pre-shot routine is designed to alert your mind and your body it is time to become totally-focused for one minute. A round of golf may take four or five hours to complete. You can't ask your mind to stay totally-focused for that period of time; however, the golf swing takes less than a minute to line up, take a few practice swings, take a stance and swing the club to strike the ball. The swing itself takes only a second or more. You can't ask your mind to stay focused for four or five hours, but you can ask it to become focused for a minute at a time. The pre-shot routine is the trigger or switch that starts this process.

Stand behind the ball and visualize sweeping the tee off the turf or driving a nail through the ball in your mind. Select a spot just a few inches or feet in front of the ball. This will help you line up the imaginary "Hitting Area". Address the ball, and take a practice swing, in slow-motion stopping the club head just before impact (the stutter swing). Now you are ready to swing the club for real. Do this before each shot on the practice range to get this routine established in the mind, and it will come automatically when you are on the golf course.

Start with the pitching wedge and ball, but only imagine the flat tee in front of the ball. You can put the glove under the armpit if you like. Place a ball on a raised tee. When a ball is on a raised tee, you should visualize a flat tee on another tee the same height as the first just a 1/4 of an inch in front of the ball. You should feel the club head sweeping the tee off the imaginary forward tee before it begins its climb skyward.

Some students have told me this trick really works for them. Off the tee they look at the front of the ball rather than the back or top of the ball. This will insure a swing that will "hit through" the ball rather than at or under the ball. If this solution sounds odd to you, think of the swing as a "karate chop". The "karate chop" never hits at the board or bricks but beyond the board or brick. This focus insures a blow that will hit through the target rather than at the target. By looking at the front of the ball, you will accomplish the same effect.

Start off in super slow-motion and build up speed. You will be surprised how far you can hit a ball in slow-motion. Build up speed until you are no longer hitting the ball solidly. As you did earlier, back the swing down until you can once again hit the ball solidly time after time.

Once you are hitting the pitching wedge solidly time-after-time, from a raised tee, lower the tee to flush in the ground and repeat the exercise. Finally, move to a place where you can set the ball (without a tee) on a nice bed of grass (a perfect lie), and hit a few ball using the pitching wedge from there. Since you will not have the tee in front of the ball, you must visualize it, and you must dig up a little dirt after you have hit the ball. If you don't take a little dirt after you have hit the ball, you are not using the Simple Swing.

The goal here is to get the pitching wedge down pat before moving on to the other clubs. If you can't hit the pitching wedge correctly, you won't be able to hit the other clubs correctly either. The pitching wedge should be the easiest club in your bag to hit, excluding the putter. This is true because the pitching wedge has a short shaft, and the shorter the shaft, the easier it is to control the club head. The same rule applies to the shorter shaft that applies to the shorter back swing.

The pitching wedge also has a club face that imparts backspin, rather than sidespin. Backspin causes a ball to go straight, and sidespin causes the ball to curve. The higher the loft (the more the club face looks toward the sky), the more backspin and less sidespin will be imparted on the ball.

Because the pitching wedge has a lot of loft on the club face and has a short shaft, you need not hit the ball perfectly in order to get the ball to travel in the direction of the target. What this means is, if the ball is not behaving correctly, you have a serious problem with your swing. Major problems will show up as you use lower-numbered clubs. (Clubs with less loft and longer shafts.)

**R**emember, the three factors that can determine the direction of a golf ball's flight:

- The direction the club face is looking when it strikes the ball.

- The direction the club face is traveling when it strikes the ball.

- A combinations of these factors.

**I**f the club face is looking at the target, the ball will go towards the target; however, if the club face is looking right when it strikes the ball, the ball may start out going straight, but the sidespin created by the open (a club face that is looking right of the target) clubface will cause the ball to curve right.

**A** closed (a club face that looks left of the target) may start out straight, but the sidespin will cause the ball to curve left.

If the club face is looking at the target, but the swing path is off line, the ball will travel in the direction of the swing path. In a moment we will discuss "the two wrongs might make a right" aspect of the swing.

If you are not hitting the ball solidly at the range, it is usually due to:

**1.** Taking too long a back swing or using to much wrist cock.
**SOLUTION:** Go back to the slow-motion drill using a short back swing and almost no wrist cock and build up speed. Remember the "Pile Driver" story. The fewer moving parts, the easier it is to keep the swing in sync.

**2.** Hitting behind the ball once the ball is on a bed of grass. This means you are back to doing the natural thing of trying to help or lift the ball into the air.
**SOLUTION**: Your job is to get the ball to go forward, let the club head get the ball into the air. Just sweep the tee. Golf is not a natural game.

**3.** Pushing balls to the right. Problem: Head and upper body are moving either upward or in front of the ball before impact.
**SOLUTION**: See club head pass under your nose before allowing your head to move. Go

back to slow-motion if necessary. Remember, the upper body rotates around your back leg - only the back knee moves forward. This way your weight and head are behind the ball at impact.

**4**. Ball curving right to left or left to right. Some ball movement is normal, especially for the six iron or seven or five wood; however, excess curves are not helpful. Problem: The club face is not looking at the target at impact. **SOLUTION**: Make sure your grip is light and try changing the ball position from the middle of your stance to a little forward or a little back.

**I**t is extremely important you be able to hit the ball perfectly straight with the pitching wedge, but you need not hit it perfectly straight with the rest of the clubs. A small amount of bend is acceptable with the eight iron; a little more bend is acceptable with the six iron, and even more bend is acceptable and even desirable with the 7 and 5 woods. The keys to the bend are consistency and controllability. If the bend in the ball is close to being the same every time, then you can control where the ball will land by adjusting your aim. If the bend is not consistent, then controlling where the ball will land is out of the question.

By the way, golf is one of the few places in this world where two wrongs might make a right. Example: If you swing the club head across the "hitting area", the ball should go left. If you strike the ball with an open club face, the ball should go right. If you do both together, one may counteract the other and cause the ball to start out left but bend to the right and end up close to where you were aiming. I tell my students if you do these same movements consistently, don't change the swing because it is results we are looking for, not form.

If you find yourself hitting such a ball, you may not wish to try to correct your swing. However, I remind you; if you do correct one of these swing faults, without correcting the other, you won't improve, but will see your game decline drastically because finding the fairway will become almost impossible.

As long as you have a pretty good idea where the ball will go when you strike it, you need not redo the swing. It is only if the swing is totally inconsistent, that you need to go back and redo the swing by swinging in slow-motion.

When you are satisfied you have the pitching wedge down pat, select the 8 iron and start the whole process all over again. Then move to the 6 iron and finally to the 7 and/or 5 wood.

Once you have worked your way down to the five wood/seven wood, spend the rest of your time at the range hitting the pitching wedge and the woods. These two or three clubs, along with the putter, will account for over 75% of your shots. You will use the 5 wood off the tee for most par 4 and par 5 holes; and, in most cases, you will use it again off the fairway or short rough for your second shot or long par 4 and par 5 holes. You will use your pitching wedge from anywhere from 60 yards into the green. You might find you can hit a pitching wedge 80 yards to a 100 yards with some roll.

After moving down through all five clubs, what do you know? Are you beginning to feel really comfortable out here? How do you feel when you don't hit the ball solidly? Are you correcting yourself on every swing? While it is great to know what you are doing wrong, it is often better to focus on what you are doing right. "I certainly hit it solidly that time, or my head was certainly back and still on that shot."

## Golf is a negative game.

This is true because your body is not a machine and thus cannot make the same movement over and over again without some degree of error. A great player like Ben Hogan was thrilled if he made a few perfect shots per round. Gary Player, only one of three people to win all four major championships, states, "golf is a game of recovery," and Lee Trevino claims, "it is not a game of who makes the best good shots, but which golfer's have the best misses."

You can't play better than you can play, but you can always play worse than you can play. Sounds simple doesn't it? But do you really understand what it means? You hit a perfect shot and then believe you should be able to hit that same shot every time. While it is good to set high standards, please don't expect to reach them on the golf course. Golf is a game of infinity. Simply learn to enjoy the game and the companionship that goes with it and don't look for perfection because the last place you will ever find perfection is on the golf course or practice range. The pros can't find it, so does it really make sense for you to expect to?

In reality, you should visualize hitting every shot perfectly before you attempt to make the shot for real, but if it doesn't turn out to be a perfect shot, take what the golf gods give you and be grateful. Never complain to yourself about how dumb the shot was or how dumb you are for hitting it or even for playing the game in the first place. Negative "self talk" can never help your game, but it can ruin your day and that of those around you.

The pros are the biggest excuse artists in the world. They take full credit for any shot that has a happy ending (like the ball hitting a cart path and bouncing or rolling and extra 50 yards towards the hole), but if they hit a poor shot, it is always due to a poor lie or a slippery grip or some other excuse. When asked about this tendency, Dave Stockton said, "We (the pros) hit so many less-than-perfect shots during a round that if we blamed ourselves for everyone of them, we would be beating up on ourselves all day long and would be totally destroyed by the end of the round." If the pros feel this way, imagine what an average golfer could do to himself, with negative self-talk, while playing 18 holes.

**Helpful Hints**

- Do not correct yourself after every swing, but wait until you have hit three bad shots in a row before you begin making any adjustments. Why hit three solid shots, then hit a poor one and feel an adjustment is in order?

**95**

- Do not rush yourself. You are only going to be at the practice range occasionally, so enjoy and learn while you are there; and for-goodness-sake take your time during the swing (never rush your golf swing), and take your time between swings.

## Checkpoints

Belly button turns and faces the ball at impact. Is the club going towards the target rather than towards the sky on the follow-through? Make sure the head stays behind the ball until the club head has made contact with the ball, and the club head has swept the imaginary tee from the "Hitting Area."

Lastly, if you are doing okay with the high-number irons but having trouble with the 6 iron or 7 or 5 wood, go back and make sure you haven't increased the speed of your swing because the odds are you have.

**Calibrate the average distance you hit each club.**
When you reach the last 20 or 25 balls (depending if you are using one wood or two) in your basket, divide them up into four groups of five. From a bed of grass hit five pitching wedges shots at the 100 yard marker and make a note of how far each went in the air. Do the same for the 8 iron, 6 iron and 7 & 5 woods only when using these clubs aim at the 150 yard marker.

It is "in the air" that is important because if you have to carry the ball over a pond for 60 yards on the course, it does you no good to know you can hit a pitching wedge 60 yards unless you know that 20 of those 60 yards are usually roll. If you know you only hit a PW 40 yards in the air, then you will also know to use the 8 iron or 6 iron to fly the ball over the 60 yards across the pond.

When you are recording distance or calibrating clubs, there is a tendency to count the maximum hit as your club's distance. Out of five shots with an eight iron say you hit one 100 yards while the rest were between 80 and 90 yards. Now you are on the course; you have 100 yards to the center of the green; and you pull out your eight iron because you know you can hit it 100 yards - if you hit it perfectly; but if you don't hit the ball perfectly, it may end up five yards short of the green with you wondering why. What you are looking for is your average distance!

When you are calibrating your club's distance, there is a tendency to try harder and therefore swing harder which, of course, does not allow you to hit the ball solidly with a relaxed swing. The results you get from trying to swing too hard will throw your calibration all out of kilter. Just swing the same way you were swinging before you reached the last 20 balls.

As you become more comfortable with the swing, you will be able to swing harder and faster and still strike the ball solidly and sweep the imaginary tee from in front of the ball. This means you will gain distance with each club. Once you have hit two or three shots over the green, you will know it is time to recalibrate you clubs once again. Once you have a pretty good idea of how far you are hitting the ball with each club, you are ready for the course.

"How can this be possible?," I am often asked. "I need hours and hours of practice before I'll be ready."

I would never discourage you from practicing, but because I know your time is limited, I have built this system on mind-memory, not muscle memory. If your subconscious mind knows what to do and can visualize it clearly, then it can make your body perform the task without a great deal of practice. If you can visualize the swing and the shot, if you can feel and swing the club head over the "Hitting Area" and sweeping the tee off the turf a 1/4 of an inch in front of the ball, then there is nothing left to do but to play the game.

This swing is not about hitting a golf ball, but about swinging the club head over the entire part of the "Hitting Area" and sweeping the imaginary flat tee in the process. If the club head travels through the "Hitting Area" and sweeps the tee, then the ball will be struck solidly and fly towards the target. What more could you ask for?

# THE COURSE

Okay, you have just taken up boxing, and your first fight is with Mike Tyson. Are you kidding me? He will kill you! Okay, so you didn't just learn to box; but if you did, would your first fight be with a former champion?

You just learned to ski. Are you now ready for the expert trail at the very top of the mountain? Again, this adventure could cause your death.

So what's the point? The point is you now know how to play golf; but just because going out to play on Pebble Beach (one of the nation's toughest courses) won't cause you bodily harm doesn't mean that is the place you should head for your first round of golf.

If I had my "druthers," your first course would be a par 3 or an executive course where most of the holes are par 3 holes. These courses can help you to develop a good, short game, and they can be played in a limited amount of time. Usually an executive course will have a practice range which will give you a chance to hit some 5 woods off the tee to make up for the long tee shots you don't get to hit on the executive course.

My second choice for your first course would be an easy course with a slope rating of a 100 or below. The slope rating will tell you how hard the course is: 115-124 is in the middle range, anything below 115

**99**

is easy. and anything above 125 can be a real challenge. You will need a course that is very short (around 6000 yards) with very little rough, sand, water, or woods. And, by the way, please play from the front tees or the first tees behind the women's tees unless you are a woman.

The English have a saying: "Rules are for the obedience of fools and the guidance of wise men." When you are first learning to play golf, do not be to concerned about the rules or the score. There are rules of golf (which I am telling you as a beginner you can bend) and there are rules of golf etiquette (which you should obey). You will learn how to get out of trouble on the course, but if you get stuck in a sand bunker and can't get out after a couple of tries, do not hesitate to pick the ball up, place it outside the bunker, and proceed playing.

The same is true if you must hit the ball 180 yards in the air to carry over the water, and you know it will take your best shot to do so. Give it a try; but if you don't carry the water, don't hesitate to simply lay a ball down on the other side of the water and continue playing. Remember your playing companions want you to play quickly, courteously, and safely. At this time your score or your obeying every rule is not important to them. Later it will be but not now, which is why we suggest you always start out by playing "Winter Rules" (roll the ball to get a perfect lie).

According to the USGA there is no such thing as "Winter Rules," yet they are played at almost every golf course in the country in the winter when the courses are not in as good a condition as they are in the other three seasons. A lot of golfers play winter rules all year round. I suggest the beginning golfer play them until they are fully confident they can hit a ball from a perfect lie. Once they can do this, then they can give their attention to hitting balls from the imperfect lies they will get on the golf course.

I am assuming you have practiced putting at home or in your office so you are a decent putter with feel and touch and will two-putt most holes. I expect you will one-putt a few greens and might three-putt a few as well. All in all, you should have the capability to shoot "bogey" golf. I didn't say you would shoot "bogey golf" only that you now had the capability to shoot "bogey golf." It might take you a few rounds of golf to get there, but you should be confident of your ability to get there.

It is recommended for your first practice round you take a good friend with you who can show you around not only the course, but the pro shop, club house, practice green and practice range. If you want to learn on your own, you can contact your local public course and ask them when would be a good time to come out and play a round of golf by your-self. I have found the public courses to be a great place to play alone if you arrive in the evening after their golf leagues have finished teeing off. Usually this is after 6:30 p.m. or so.

Your friend should be aware of this book and agree to help you out with rules, etiquette, shots to get out of trouble, and help in reading the greens (which way the ball will break). He or she should also be willing to refrain from giving you advice regarding your swing because they will only tell you how to swing like a pro.

The three places you will want to visit before you reach the first tee are: The pro shop, the practice range, and the practice green.

At the pro shop you will pay your fee and decide if you will use a riding cart, rent a pull cart, or carry your own bag. If they have a caddie program, you have started your golf experience at the wrong course because this course is not the place for a beginner. If your friend doesn't know, the pro will be happy to tell you where the distance markers are and what they look like. He will also tell you where you can and can't take the riding cart.

## THE PRACTICE RANGE (at the course)

At the practice range your goal is to warm up and to get the right tempo (tick-tock) of the swing. You are to go through your pre-shot routine before you hit each ball on the range. If you do it on the range, you will do it on the course, and you need it on the course to keep you focused and relaxed. The range is also a great place to relieve some of the tension that will occur with your first time on the course. Don't forget about your Square Breathing Technique. You may not have the time to go through the entire practice range routine, but you should start with the pitching wedge and work your way down to the 5 wood. Make your last few swings on the range with the 5 wood off a tee just barely off the ground because this will simulate your first tee shot off the first tee.

## THE PRACTICE GREEN

On the putting green start out by making a few three foot putts; then work your way further and further away from the hole. Lag putting is just as important as making those three footers. To alter the practice, place four balls in a direct line, spaced about a foot apart, with the first ball being three feet from the hole. Try to make all four balls in a row before you move the balls to another side of the hole. This exercise will provide you with some pressure which will get you use to the pressure of the course. It will also make you a better putter.

You can't make many putts that curve or break unless you can make the "straight in" putts first. Your practice at the home or office was designed to build your confidence in your ability to make the straight in putt. If you wish to build this confidence even further, I might suggest you bring about six feet of string with you to the course. At the pro shop pick up two short scoring pencils. Tie the string to the top of these pencils. On the practice green locate a hole that allows a straight in putt (a putt with no break on the way to the hole). Your friend can help you locate such a spot. Stick one pencil into the ground just beyond the hole and stretch the string over the hole and back to a spot six feet from the hole and place the other pencil in the ground. This string should now be about 1 1/2 to 2 inches above the ground and form a very tight line to the hole. Place the ball directly under the string, about six inches in front of the pencil, furthest from the hole.

The string will now provide you a direct line to

the hole. If you can keep the ball rolling under the string, it will surely go in the hole providing you get the ball to the hole and without so much force it jumps over the hole. The string will also provide you with a guide for your putter to go straight back (directly under the string) and then straight through. If the putter gets off line you will know it right away. Finally, placing the ball only six inches in front of the pencil prevents you from taking too long a backswing, because if you do, you will hit the pencil. This exercise forces you to focus on the power of the forward stoke, rather than the backswing.

You want to spend some time with this exercise; and then when you find yourself on the green with a straight in putt, you will be able to visualize the string and simply roll the ball under it as you sink the putt.

**R**emember, all putts are stroked as if they were "straight in" putts. That is to say, if the ball will break two balls to the left, you should aim at a spot two balls to the right of the hole and putt towards that spot as if it were the hole.

### How to read a green
First and foremost, ask your friends for help. When your friends tells you which way the ball will break on its way to the hole, ask them how they came to that conclusion and listen carefully to their reply. You are not permitted to do this when you are playing a regular game, using USGA rules.

# OUT OF TROUBLE WITH A LITTLE HELP FROM YOUR FRIENDS

## Trouble shots

You already know how to hit 90% of the shots required in the golf game, but there are a few shots we haven't covered. Some golf courses are loaded with tall grass, sand, water, trees, and hills. If you follow my suggestion, your first few courses shouldn't have many of these hazards on them. Furthermore, your simple swing, which puts the emphasis on accuracy, not power, is designed to keep you out of most hazards.

Having said this, you may occasionally find yourself in one of these situations, so you should be prepared to deal with them.

Most instructional books will go through each type of lie and explain how you are to adjust your body and your swing to accommodate each shot. Because your simple swing has a compact backswing, it is ideally suited to help you escape from trouble without a lot of modification.

When you find yourself in trouble, your first priority must be to get out of trouble, <u>using only one shot</u>. This is true even if it means playing the ball away from the hole. Do not make the mistake of the average golfer, who tries to pull off an unsuccessful low percentage escape shot, only to find the ball still in trouble for his next shot.

In fairway bunkers (sand) you must choose a club with enough loft in the club face to insure the ball will fly over the lip of the bunker. To achieve distance with this shot, the club face must strike the ball before it strikes the sand. Also, make sure your feet are buried deep in the sand, and thus you are standing on solid ground. Since this may put you closer to the ball, you may find it necessary to grip down on the club a little.

There are only two major trouble shots that require a major adjustment in our approach to the ball; greenside bunkers (sand) and tall grass. Both of these shots require the club face to strike behind the ball.

"Greenside bunkers are easy," say the pros. "All you need to do is open your stance, open up the blade of your sand wedge, alter you normal swing by swinging across the target line and strike the sand two inches behind the ball and finish with a high follow-through."

If you are willing to spend the time practicing this shot, then do it the way the pros tell you to do it; however, there are a few options that don't require time and practice. Option number one is to use the putter and putt out of the greenside bunker if the bunker is a shallow one. This method might not get the ball to stop near the hole, but it should guarantee your first objective, which is to get the ball out of trouble in one shot.

The second option is to use one of the newer sand

wedges with a very large, flat sole or flange. If you are going to play courses with sand, you need a sand wedge just like you need a putter once you get the ball on the green. These new high-tech sand wedges allow you to forget all about opening up the club face, opening up your stance, or changing your swing to cut across the target line. Instead, all you need to do is dig your feet into the sand for a firm stance and swing normally. Your only requirements are to hit a couple inches behind the ball and to keep the club head moving to a follow-through. In other words, don't be timid; be aggressive!

If you need to throw the ball a good distance then finish with a high, follow-through. If the hole is close to the trap, use a short follow-through although I do recommend for starters you always go for the center of the green regardless of where the pin (hole) is located. The club face will throw the sand into the air, and the ball will ride the sand. Your club face should never touch the ball, only the sand, for this shot.

Most courses, which have a lot of greenside bunkers, will also have a practice bunker in addition to their practice green and practice range. USE IT! If you don't have a new, hi-tech sand wedge, use a regular one and imagine the ball is sitting on a tee that is buried under the sand. Don't focus on the ball but rather try to cut that buried tee in half with the sand wedge. If the course is crowded, never take more than two strokes trying to get out of the sand bunker. Simply pick the ball up and go to the next hole or use the old hand wedge and throw the ball on to the green. Don't cry; we have all been there when we were just learning the game.

I have seen a lot of beginners try to play golf without a sand wedge in their bag. If you are going to play on a course that has sand bunkers, don't do this. You can't putt without a putter, and you shouldn't try to escape a sand bunker without a sand wedge.

In tall grass around the green, you will use the same sand wedge and the same shot; however, the clubface will not dig into the ground but will slide under the ball as it is sitting on the thick grass. For this shot, the clubface will strike the ball and will act much like the snowplow we talked about earlier in the book. Again, for long shots, make a long follow-through, and for shorter shots make a shorter follow-through. The heavy weight of the sand wedge will help the club cut through the thick grass.

With both of these shots you must avoid the temptation of abandoning your simple, compact swing for a longer, more powerful, full swing. As stated before, a fuller, longer, swing might provide more power but will not let you control the club head of the club as well. On these shots, as with regular shots, making the club head do what it is supposed to do is far more important than a powerful stroke that cuts through the sand or the grass incorrectly.

**I**n tall grass (rough) away from the green. If the ball finds tall grass away from the green, use a 7 or 5 wood and execute the shot in the same manner as above. The 7 or 5 wood will slide more easily through the tall grass than an iron because it is more rounded. However, if the ball is really buried in the rough, the 7 or 5 wood may not be able to get to the ball in which case you must revert back to the sand wedge and just bump the ball back into the fairway.

## IN THE WIND

I really do not advise playing golf in anything but perfect weather conditions, at least for beginners. You want golf to be fun, and you have a lot to do without fighting inclement weather or high winds. However, there are places in the world, including some places in the U.S. where if you want to play golf you must play in the wind. When it is breezy, swing easy. The harder you hit the ball, the higher it will fly into the wind. Once the wind gets a hold of the ball, the wind is in control of the shot, not you. To keep the ball low, use lower numbered clubs than usual. Example: When the wind is in your face and you would normally use an 8 iron, use a 6.

### "A Little Help from Your Friends"

I started this section out by having you ask a friend to help you around the course. I stated your friend should be willing to help you in certain areas and refrain from helping in others. Bonding with friends, family members and business associates is a big part of golf. People like to help people, and bonding takes place when help is either given or received. It is with this thought in mind we have tried to provide enough places for people to help you without interfering with your swing.

Helping you with reading greens, with rules, with etiquette, how to bet using a handicap, how to hit out of trouble, and how to play in inclement weather are all areas where you should welcome advice.

Where you must resist your friends help or advice is in how to swing a golf club, because they will try to get you to swing the club the way the pros do and any effort on your part to do so will more than likely lead to inconsistent shots regardless of their good intentions.

# EQUIPMENT

People will say you can't buy a better game. They will be misleading you. There are hundreds of club makers throughout the world, and each has a staff of researchers trying to invent new ways to make a golf club that will allow the poorer player to play better. Ping, Taylor Made, Titleist, King Cobra and Callaway are just a few of the companies that have succeeded in making the game more playable and thus more enjoyable for the less than skilled players. The touring pros are not always happy with these advancements because they want the player's skill to do the job, not the equipment. However, Senior Tour players seem to welcome the improvements. Most of the Senior Tour players are hitting the ball farther today then they did when they were twenty years younger playing on the regular tour.

The point is do not play golf with outdated equipment. The clubs of today are light years ahead of the golf clubs of yesterday - as far as the everyday or casual golfer is concerned.

The new equipment has larger heads making it is easier to hit or harder to miss the ball. They have perimeter weighted heads to give the clubs a larger sweet spot. Hits off the toe or heel of the club will still fly straight and long. Graphite shafts are available to help those who need it to get more distance. And finally, there are the high-tech Sand Wedges that do most of the work for you.

**I**f you want to go "first class" and impress your friends and business associates, then get the equipment from the leading club manufactures; however, I have found some great clubs made by lesser-known companies that are sold in discount stores. Just make sure the clubs are oversized and perimeter weighted.

**Balls:** When you first start out, play with used balls (recycled balls fished out of ponds or lakes on the course) or XXX out balls. They will play just as well and fly just as far as new balls, and you won't feel so bad or waste a lot of time looking for them should you hit one astray. Just make sure they are two piece balls. The three piece balls are what the pros us. They spin a lot, which means they curve a lot in flight and they also cut (need to be replaced) very easily. You can save the new balls until you want to impress your business associates at the club.

**Shoes:** If you are going to play at a country club, you will need spikes; however, Sam Snead used to practice in his bare feet. He claimed without spikes, he was forced to focus on balance. Spikes are not necessary to play golf. Sneakers will do just fine providing the golf course does not require spikes. Some courses claim spikes help maintain the greens by punching holes in the turf and letting the grass breath. Other courses claim the spikes actually hurt the greens, and demand that golfers replace their spikes with the new soft spikes.

# SUMMARY

I hope what you have read and experienced as a result of this book has made sense to you. If you understand what needs to be done and understand why it needs to be done (the belief system), then doing it becomes extremely easy. This is especially true if you used positive visualization and then do the exercises as described.

As you have gone through this book, you probably said to yourself, "he has already said this once or twice, how many times does he need to say it"? The truth is, I have tried to say the same thing over and over many times but in many different ways in order that your mind would absorb the new material as effortlessly as possible.

If a beginning golfer realizes Golf is not a Natural Game, and understands the importance of developing touch and understands that his or her role is to get the ball to go forward with a solid blow, not a hard blow, as the club head sweeps the imagery tee from in front of the ball while driving the club head through the "hitting area", then I would say you understand the key message "Instant Golf" is trying to deliver.

Develop a great short game and a consistent golf swing by using an abbreviated backswing and sweeping the ball off the turf rather than picking or lifting it, and you have *Instant Golf* in a nutshell.

If you know you are not going to swing like a pro because you started playing the game too late in life, and you realize spending time and money on lessons and at the practice range won't really help either, then when others try to help you with your game by telling you or showing you how to swing like a pro, you will be able to resist the temptation to try their advice.

If you are willing to invest a few hours in the beginning of your golf life to get down a few sound principles, then you will be spared the ordeal of trying to learn everything by trial and error. For those of you who have been playing golf for awhile but without a great deal of success, let me say you may find you needed to work at these exercises a little harder than a beginner because you are trying to break old habits and beginners have no old habits to break.

I can tell you this. You already know twice as much about golf as half the players on the course. To prove this point, simply observe some of the poorer players you see on the course. Notice their long backswings on short shots; notice their desire to help the ball into the air; notice how they swing harder with the woods than with the irons; and notice their huge backswings and how the ball flies out of control off the club face as a result of such a long backswing. Notice that their tempo is always set on hurry. These sobering thoughts may not relieve all the tension in your swing, but they should relieve enough of it that you might swing the clubs as freely as you did in your yard or at the range.

I did not promise to make you a club champion or to put you on the PGA tours. What I did promise you was to show you the stepping stones between the land of the beginners and the island of Solid, Respectable Golfers.

You are going to surprise yourself and your friends with how quickly you can play a respectable game of golf. There are many ways to play golf and many ways to swing a golf club. I believe *Instant Golf* is the easiest to learn and the most consistent; but it certainly isn't the only way, and if you really get hooked on the game and want to devote more time to it, you may want to take a more aggressive approach to help you reach that next level. Always remember, you can at anytime return and reread this book if you start to go backwards rather than forward in your golf game.

Unfortunately, the law that states, "If you want to swing and play like a pro you must learn and practice like a pro and if you didn't learn like a pro you can't expect to swing like one" will always be in effect and nothing you do can will change this law. However, golfers who started late and have short backswings have confidence they can pull a critical shot off when needed. Golfers, with long backswings, who didn't learn before 30, can only hope they can pull a particular shot off when the game is on the line. Which golfer will you be?

I welcome your comments. Write me at, PO Box 666, West Chester, Ohio 45069 or phone 513-777-7231.